ALSO BY SYLVIA BOORSTEIN

It's Easier Than You Think:
The Buddhist Way to Happiness

Don't Just Do Something, Sit There:
A Mindfulness Retreat

That's Funny, You Don't Look Buddhist:
On Being a Faithful Jew and a Passionate Buddhist

Pay Attention, for Goodness' Sake

Practicing the Perfections
of the Heart—The Buddhist
Path of Kindness

Sylvia Boorstein

BALLANTINE BOOKS • NEW YORK

A Ballantine Book
Published by The Ballantine Publishing Group
Copyright © 2002 by Sylvia Boorstein

www.ballantinebooks.com

Library of Congress Cataloging-in-Publication Data

Boorstein, Sylvia.
    Pay attention, for goodness' sake : Buddhist practice of kindness /
Sylvia Boorstein.
        p.   cm.
        1. Paramitas (Buddhism) 2. Perfection—Religious life—
Buddhism. 3. Religious life—Buddhism. I. Title

BQ4336 .B66 2002
294.3'5—dc21   2002018483

ISBN 0-345-44810-3

Manufactured in the United States of America

First Edition: September 2002

Designed by C. Linda Dingler

10 9 8 7 6 5 4 3 2 1

*The venerable Ananda, a senior disciple of the Buddha,
spoke of noble friendship as being "half of the holy life."
The Buddha said, "No, Ananda. It is not.
It is the whole of the holy life."*

*This book is for my noble friends.
Some appear in stories, mentioned by name.
Others, because they have supported my heart
and held my hand as this book was being born,
will recognize themselves in what I've written.
~Thank you, all.*

Contents

Contents

Contents

Contents

Promising Signs

My first Mindfulness retreat experience—a Friday-afternoon-to-Sunday-evening residential weekend for twenty students—happened in the spring of 1977 in a private home in a suburb of San Jose, California. Everything about it was difficult. I didn't know anyone. It was hot. We sat for meditation crowded together in what must have been formerly a storage shed, now serving as a meditation room in the backyard. We slept on mattresses too close together on the floors of the bedrooms, men and women sharing rooms, dressing and undressing—albeit speedily and discreetly—all at the same time. I felt shy and confused. I was also in pain because no one had told me there wouldn't be any coffee and I had a huge caffeine-withdrawal headache. I sat on my meditation bench counting first the hours and then the minutes remaining until the time my husband was scheduled to pick me up. I rehearsed the long, indignant speeches I planned to make on the drive home about how poorly he had prepared me for this event and what nonsense it all was.

Two months later, on July 7, I was on a plane en route to Portland, Oregon, enrolled in another, even longer Mindfulness retreat, the second of many, many retreats that continue even now and have become—although I couldn't have imagined it then—a core element of my spiritual life. When people ask me now, "How come, given that your first experience was so difficult, you went back?" I respond, in all candor, "I'm not sure. It's mysterious. Maybe it's grace."

I have only two clues. One is a photograph, a 3½-by-5-inch black-and-white class-graduation-style photo, of all twenty of us and our teacher grouped together in three rows facing a camera, probably taken on Sunday in the late afternoon. I am sitting in the front row, at the very right end. I am smiling. Looking at this picture now, I think that perhaps I'd had more hints of promise than I recall. Perhaps my mind, in its normal self-protective mode—remembering discomfort in order to avoid further discomfort—began retelling itself exaggerated stories of pain in a voice loud enough to drown out the whispers of hope. The other clue is a clear recollection of a decorative plaque on the mantelpiece of the living room, a highly polished redwood burl with a sentence etched into it, the kind people buy in souvenir shops in national parks. Usually those plaques say HOME SWEET HOME or SISTERS ARE FRIENDS FOREVER. I think it was the message on this plaque that brought me back. It read LIFE IS SO DIFFICULT, HOW CAN WE BE ANYTHING BUT KIND?

Pay Attention,
for Goodness' Sake

The Paramitas

/ / / / / / / / / / / / / / / / / / / /

GOODNESS AND KINDNESS

My friend Lew Richmond took ill suddenly and almost died of viral encephalitis. Lew and I are longtime members of a Buddhist teacher-colleague group that he named Rhinoceros for what he saw as our common tendency to stake out independent paths. At a Rhino meeting just a few days after Lew's crisis had passed, several of the group members, reassured that he would live, admitted to having begun to compose his eulogy. We mentioned his many talents. Lew is a Zen teacher. And a pianist. And a composer. And an author. And a lecturer.

/ / / /

And a business consultant who is the CEO of his own computer design company.

"The best thing about Lew, though," Jack said, "is that he is a truly good person."

Roger laughed. "Do you suppose," he said, "that after all our sophisticated Buddhist discussions, and all our meditation practice, and all our teaching, that what it's all about is being a *truly good person*?"

I do.

The Buddha was a profoundly good person. He was generous and moral, restrained and patient, honest and openhearted. He was also tough. He did not confuse compassion with passivity. He obligated monks and nuns to leave the community when their presence was disruptive. In one of his earlier incarnations he killed a murderer, out of compassion, to spare him the pain he would suffer in later lifetimes for the heinous crime he was about to commit. He acted wisely and energetically, out of love, on behalf of all beings.

We could too.

Most of the meditators I know began their practice hoping for special and exotic experiences. I was hoping to lessen—perhaps even erase—my perception of pain in the world. Instead, my sense of the suffering in the world deepened. What surprised me were the experiences of awe and wonder and appreciation that made the suffering bearable. What surprised me even more was that dedication to goodness—dedication in response to an inner moral mandate rather than external restraint—was both the antidote to the pain and the source of great happiness.

When people ask the Dalai Lama, "Is Buddhism a religion?" he answers, "Yes, it is." Then they ask, "What kind of religion is it?" He responds, "My religion is kindness."

You might think, "*Everyone's* is."

Everyone's is. That's true. It's not complicated to describe the goal of a spiritual life. It's easier than you think to explain it. It's more difficult than you can imagine to do it.

A magazine journalist interviewed me on the telephone for an article about newly emerging religious forms. He wanted to know what I thought about people "mixing and matching religions."

I responded (clearly disingenuously, given that I am both a Buddhist teacher and an observant Jew), "Are people doing that?"

The interviewer said, "Yes, indeed. People are just taking what they like and making up their own religions. Like salad religions—a little bit of this, a little bit of that—whatever they like, they mix it in. Do you think it's bad or good?"

I said, "Well, I don't know if it's bad or good. If people are doing it, maybe it's a reflection of what the psychoanalyst Erik Erikson called the American character. He believed we are inspired by what we think of as the pioneer spirit, like cowboys—independent, able to go out on the range alone, taking the best of what's available and making it work. And maybe it also means that people are realizing that what seemed important to them in their life—materialism and consumerism—doesn't work at all to make a happy heart. It actually makes an unhappy heart. And an unhappy world. And maybe people are discovering that they really need something that speaks to the essence of their being, something that connects them directly, with conscious intention, to the truth of their experience so that their lives become meaningful. Maybe it is a good thing."

He said, "But do you think it could be dangerous?"

I said, "I don't know if it could be dangerous. I suppose there might be a pitfall."

"What would the pitfall be?"

I replied, "Well, if you were in a religion all by yourself, you would have nobody to encourage you if you were making progress, to tell you, 'That's great.' And you also wouldn't have anybody to tell you that you were deluding yourself and that nothing was happening."

Then he asked, "What's supposed to happen?"

"What's supposed to *happen*? What's supposed to happen is that our vision becomes transformed. We begin to see, with increasing clarity, how much confusion and suffering there is in our own minds and hearts, and we also see the ways in which our own personal suffering creates suffering in the world. That part is heartbreaking. And totally daunting. But that's not all. We also get to see the extraordinariness of life, how amazing it is that life exists and continually re-creates itself in an incredible, spectacular, mind-boggling, lawful way. When we see clearly, our awe and our thanksgiving for the very fact that life is happening makes it impossible to do anything other than address the pain in the world, to try to heal it, to hope never to add one single extra drop of pain or suffering to it. As our understanding increases, our hearts become more responsive. We become the compassionate people we were meant to be. That's the whole point of practice. *That's* what's supposed to happen."

There was a very long pause, because I had gone from measured, thoughtful teacher to thundering preacher in about thirty seconds.

Then he said, "Very good!"

It *is* good. The Buddha called the message he taught "good medicine." It's medicine with two active ingredients. One ingredient is a set of lifestyle choices—how we act, how we speak, how we work, how we manage our relationships—that produces a contented heart. The other is a program of practices for paying attention that develop the direct, personal experience of the end of suffering, the liberating awareness of the changing nature of all experience, the absolute trust in the interconnectedness of everything in creation that makes every single act important and means that each of us makes a difference. I'm grateful to the journalist who asked, "What's supposed to happen?" I got to hear how passionately I believe that paying attention—Mindfulness—shows itself as goodness and kindness, as concern for others, as concern for the whole world. *That's* what this book is about. *That's* what I most want to teach.

THE BUDDHA'S PRACTICE

Accounts of the Buddha's life normally begin with his birth as Siddhartha Gautama in 563 B.C. in northern India, and continue with accounts of his childhood, his marriage, his renunciation of his life as a prince in response to his awareness of life's suffering, his vision of a monk free of suffering, and his own desire for that freedom. The central point of these accounts is always the experience known as his enlightenment—his experience, after many years of intense meditation practice as a monk, of deeply understanding the habits of mind that create suffering and, through that understanding, freeing his own mind of those habits forever. The Buddha called his understanding Dharma (the truth, the meaning of things), and he taught it for forty years. Over the centuries his message spread through Asia, became incorporated into the religious understanding and practices in many countries there, and served as the basis for the different forms of Buddhism that have continued to develop throughout the world.

Legends about the Buddha also include stories of the many previous lifetimes of Siddhartha Gautama—including prehuman incarnations in which he was an incredibly patient buffalo or a tirelessly compassionate bird—in which he perfected ten particular qualities of heart that laid the foundation for his later Buddhahood. Those same Paramitas (Perfections of the Heart) were said to be the qualities that he naturally and effortlessly manifested and radiated all the rest of his life.

The stories of the Buddha's complete understanding and totally perfected heart inspire me enormously, however incomplete and unperfected my own understanding and practice may be. The stories of his many, many years—indeed, lifetimes—of intense practice empower my own resolve.

I don't think about having total understanding forever. I think about having enlightened moments, instances in which I see clearly and choose wisely. I think about those moments becoming more frequent, more habitual. I think of how much happier my life is becoming as I make wiser choices, and that's enough.

I don't think about arriving at a totally perfected heart either. I am, however, tremendously glad to have the Paramitas as a spiritual practice, because they are ways of behaving, and although I am not in charge of what I think, I am—most of the time—responsible for how I act. Someone said recently in a class discussion of the Paramitas, "How it works for me is that my mind thinks whatever it thinks, and then my heart decides what I'll do." It's wonderful to know we can do that. It's also wonderful to think that practicing kind-hearted response is habit-forming. Short of perfection, it's enough.

Here's the list of the Paramitas:

Introduction: The Paramitas

Generosity

Morality

Renunciation

Wisdom

Energy

Patience

Truthfulness

Determination

Lovingkindness

Equanimity

I love this list.

I love knowing that all of these qualities are the natural, built-in inclinations of the human heart. We aren't born with the inclination to play the violin, or tap-dance, or do needlepoint. We have the physical equipment (ears, arms, eyes, hands, feet) and the mental equipment (memory and sometimes talent) to learn all of those skills. My sense, though, is that in cultures where those activities aren't done, no one thinks about doing them. Human beings, however, do not need lessons in friendliness. We are relational. When we aren't frightened into self-absorption, we look out for each other. We take care of each other.

And I love it that all of these qualities seem like gifts

that people give each other. Perhaps Generosity, the first of the Paramitas, most immediately evokes the idea of giving something to someone else, but I think *all* the Paramitas are gifts. And they are mutual gifts—the givers *and* the receivers benefit.

When we act morally, we give the people we meet the gift of safety, and—untroubled by the pain of guilt—we experience what the Buddha called "the bliss of blamelessness." By practicing Renunciation, we give ourselves the double gift of modulated desires (itself a relief) and—as a surprise, like the toy in the box that makes the Crackerjack even sweeter—an increased appreciation of what we already have. Think of successful renunciates in twelve-step programs—people who have given up a way of life that didn't work well for them—inspiring people newly contemplating a different life in the same way that the sight of a monk, free of suffering, inspired the Buddha to become a renunciate and then offer his life of teaching as a gift to others.

Imagine how our lives might be if everyone had even a bit more of the Wisdom that comes from seeing clearly. Suppose people everywhere, simultaneously, stopped what they were doing and paid attention for only as long as it took to recognize their shared humanity. Surely the heartbreak of the world's pain, visible to all, would convert everyone to kindness. What a gift that would be.

And think for a moment about how easy it is to feel other people's energy levels. I imagine we are all mood antennas. Everyone's personal energy level changes all the time, of course, but some people seem naturally able to transmit—by word or deed or even vibe—uplifting messages. Celia, one of the clerks in my local Safeway market, seems able—regardless of the news of the day or the mood in the store—to consistently broadcast this message: "Take heart! Life is good." She initiates conversations, even as she scans my groceries, that indicate her interest in me—something as easy as "How are you?" Our meetings always leave me cheerful. I think Celia keeps her own Energy strong by using every possible moment to connect.

Patient people enjoy the pleasure of saying to whoever is feeling anxious about delays—restaurant servers, clerks waiting on the telephone to get your credit card verified, dry cleaners who were *sure* your sweater would be ready—"It's okay. These things happen." Patience, in a rushed world, is a shared relief. Witnesses to patient transactions, as well as participants, all get to calm down.

Truthfulness levels the playing field by giving everyone involved the benefit of equal information. The very act of telling, truthfully, as much as we know makes it clear that we feel safe and establishes us as a friend. I think of friendships as relationships without guile in which people give each other the gift of intimacy.

Lovingkindness depends on forgiveness. It definitely works reciprocally. When I am able to forgive myself—which is not always easy—I am kinder to everyone. Including myself.

And we demonstrate Equanimity for each other. Imagine this scene: At the midpoint of a retreat at Spirit Rock Meditation Center, where I teach, I am part of a group of ten or so people walking silently, as we do in retreat, to the dining hall for lunch. We all stop, as if by tacit mutual decision, to admire a family of two adult quail and twelve very new babies successfully managing to cross the road, watching the father and mother quail scurry and squawk back and forth until they have accounted for all of their babies. There are giggles all around. I am thinking—and guessing that the folks around me are also thinking—"This is amazing! Quail can count!" And I'm also guessing—since we *are* midway through the retreat and we are all surely in touch with our personal sorrow—that in that moment, our capacity to appreciate quail is sharing space with whatever pain is in each of our hearts. We know it about ourselves. We intuit it about each other because we all have the same heart. And we are all, in that moment, just fine. Nothing needs to be said. We go on to lunch, having reminded each other that the heart can hold *everything* in it, that Equanimity is possible. Peace is possible.

CONTEMPORARY PRACTICE

Accounts of the Buddha's life, said to have been told by generations of disciples before they were written down and codified as scripture, often begin with the words "Thus I have heard . . . ," which carry the sense of oral tradition into the present. The teacher-to-student, elder-to-novice tone of the narratives invites us into a centuries-old community of storytellers who made the Buddha's practice their own practice. We are in the line of people who heard the story.

The sermon called Setting into Motion the Wheel of Truth is the account of the Buddha's first formal teaching after he declared his enlightenment, his experience of deeply understanding both the cause of and the remedy for suffering. It includes, before the Buddha's statement of the Four Noble Truths as the summary of his insight, the fact that he gave this teaching to five monks he met walking near Benares. A story told about that encounter describes how the five monks, recognizing the Buddha from afar as the person who had formerly done ascetic practice with them, said disparaging things to each other about him. As one account has it: "They agreed among themselves, 'Here comes the monk Gautama, who became self-indulgent, gave up the struggle and reverted to luxury,'" and only reluctantly agreed to listen to him. That same account describes how at the end of the Buddha's teaching, as one after another of the monks understood the truth of what he had said, "the news traveled right up to the Brahma world. This ten-thousand-fold world-element shook and quaked and trembled while a great measureless light surpassing the splendor of the gods appeared in the world."

The stories my friends and I tell each other about our experience of hearing the Four Noble Truths for the first time resemble, though in twenty-first-century English-language idiom, the account of what happened in Benares. My view that I was stuck with my worrying, fearful, often sorrowful mind—the victim of whatever events my life had in store for me—"shook and quaked" at the news that a liberated mind, a mind at ease in wisdom and filled with compassion, was a possibility.

Long before I had any confidence that I would be able to see clearly, it was thrilling just to know that it was possible for human beings—like the Buddha, who was a human being—to become, through practice, free of suffering.

When I teach the Four Noble Truths, I say them this way:

I. Life is challenging. For *everyone*. Our physical bodies, our relationships—*all* of our life circumstances—are fragile and subject to change. We are always accommodating.

II. The cause of suffering is the mind's struggle in response to challenge.

III. The end of suffering—a nonstruggling, peaceful mind—is a possibility.

IV. The program—the Eightfold Path—for ending suffering is:

    1. Wise Understanding: realizing the cause of suffering

    2. Wise Intention: motivation—inspired by understanding—to end suffering

    3. Wise Speech: speaking in a way that cultivates clarity

    4. Wise Action: behaving in ways that maintain clarity

5. Wise Livelihood: supporting oneself in a whole-some way
6. Wise Effort: cultivating skillful (peaceful) mind habits
7. Wise Concentration: cultivating a steady, focused, ease-filled mind
8. Wise Mindfulness: cultivating alert, balanced at-tention

Each time I teach the Four Noble Truths I reinspire myself. They make so much sense. Every step of the practice path is an ordinary, everyday activity of human beings. I say, "Look what a feedback loop this is! It's a never-ending, self-supporting system. Any piece of it builds all the other parts of it. The more we understand the causes of suffering, the greater our intention, the wiser and more compassionate our behavior, the clearer our minds, the deeper our understanding of suffering, the stronger our intention, over and over and on and on." I especially like to teach the steps in this one-through-eight progression, because I always want to pause and emphasize Wise Mindfulness. It reaffirms for me the goal of practice. Paying attention, seeing clearly in every mo-ment, leads—by way of insight—to appropriate *response*.

I sometimes end a Four Noble Truths teaching by saying, "That was a lot of words. But truly, what the

Buddha taught was simple: When we see clearly, we behave impeccably." If I want to be sure that I've made the point that acting wisely and compassionately is the inevitable, passionate imperative of the heart that comes from realizing the depth of suffering in the world, that we pay attention *for goodness' sake,* I say it this way: "When we see clearly, we behave impeccably, out of love, on behalf of all beings."

THE JOURNEY OF A LIFETIME

It's clear to me that my journey from confusion to clarity and from closed heart to open heart is one of continual arrivals and departures, a lifelong process that happens over and over again, every day. I'm fine with that. I love the story of the Buddha's enlightenment. It inspires me in the way that heroic stories are meant to inspire. The message of the story—that arriving at freedom and happiness is a possibility—reminds me that I too can arrive, even if it is again and again rather than once and for all, at that experience of clarity in which I am happy. It's easy to forget. I think of myself as always being one mind-moment away from forgetting. My experience is that we all are that way. I think, "One false move . . ."

My friends Davine and Alan planned to fly from Los Angeles to San Francisco, staying overnight just one night, to attend a party celebrating the publication of our friend Jack Kornfield's new book. The next day I phoned Jack from Lake Tahoe, where I was on holiday, to ask about the book party. "It was lovely," he said, "but Davine and Alan didn't come. Davine had food poisoning."

I called Davine. "It was *terrible*," she said. "It must have been the sandwich I ate in the airport before we took off. The flight was less than an hour, but I was so sick when we landed, I could barely stagger off the plane. Someone called the paramedics, and the paramedics called an ambulance, and on the way to the hospital, while they were setting up an IV, I felt so bad I pleaded, 'Please don't let me die,' and a very confident voice said, 'You'll be fine. You won't die,' and I believed him."

Davine and I talked about her ordeal for a long time. I was glad she wanted to talk about it. After a scare, just as after a nightmare, telling the details over and over to other people relieves the tension of a frightened mind. It's good therapy. We talked about what was in the sandwich, we talked about how kind the hospital personnel were, we talked about the efforts

Davine had made to alert the airport food concession to what had happened so that other people would not have the same experience. We talked about how you never know, *really,* where you're going. You *think* you are on your way to a party, but you end up in the emergency room. We talked about how faith sustains hope, and wondered if Davine's body had been healed by the ambulance attendant's confidence as well as by the medical treatment she had. And we talked about grace. Davine said, "How glad I am that this was a short flight and there was a hospital nearby. It could have been otherwise." What magic it is, we decided, bodies being as fragile as they are, that we last as long as most of us do. We both felt gladdened, uplifted, by that thought.

"You want to know the silliest thing?" Davine asked just as we were about to hang up.

"Sure," I said.

"Well, the next day, when I was home and better, I was mad because I weighed myself and I'd only lost a half a pound, and I'd thought for *sure* five pounds!"

We both laughed.

It *is* the silliest thing. But it's true. We have moments of such clarity, of such appreciation of the incredible web of interconnected events that carry us from breath to breath, day to day, as long as we live—and the next moment we fret about how much we weigh. Or who didn't send a Valentine. Or who forgot to compliment the dinner. Or *whatever*.

I think a lot about Big Mind–Small Mind, expansive, wide-lens consciousness and contracted, introverted consciousness. I have moments—we all do—when just being alive is a pleasure and a miracle. They feel like moments when the shutters of the mind are open and I can look out. It also feels as if those same shutters have no hooks to fix them in an open position. One small wind and *bang*—they slam shut.

My friend Rachel was visiting me for several days at my home in northern California. We spent part of our time together working, planning some meditation programs. As we worked, Rachel taught me how to identify birds. Rachel is an experienced birdwatcher, and before her visit I had been only peripherally aware of birds in my area. Her binoculars and her instructions opened a new world for me. I was thrilled.

We were having dinner on my deck, talking about the work we'd accomplished, feeling pleased, enjoying the food and each other's company, saying how blessed we both felt at that moment for our friendship and our lives. Then the phone rang. My daughter Emily wanted to tell me the latest details of my grandson Collin's upcoming bar mitzvah. All good news. At the end of our brief conversation she said, "Oh, I got a response card back from Cousin So-and-So. They aren't coming."

Bang! My mind shutters slammed shut. I thought, "It's not right! They should have come! Especially after we went to so many of *their* happy occasions!" Of course I said nothing to Emily, concluded the conversation appropriately, and then heard myself think, "Just wait until they invite me to their *next* occasion. I won't go. *Then* they'll feel sorry." Five seconds later, on my way back to the deck to rejoin Rachel, I realized that I had reflexively—but not wisely—traded an open, happy mind for a constricted, painful one. I told myself the truth: "Of *course* I'll go when I'm invited. I always go. I'm *supposed* to go. I am an elder in this clan, and the clan is spread all over, and weddings and bar mitzvahs are clan meetings, and I'll go." I could feel my mind relax, my happy mood return.

Rachel said, "Who phoned?"

I said, "It was Emmy with bar mitzvah news. Want to hear the silly thing my mind just did?"

Rachel said, "Sure."

I told her, and we both laughed.

‑‑‑‑

We laughed because we both know that this is the reflexive, instinctive response of the mind to disappointment. I sometimes think that no matter how glorious the mood, we are always one millimeter away from being trapped by anger. Or greed. Or whatever. Trapped in something. Reborn into suffering.

When I think about the point of practice I think about being able, when my mind and heart are kidnapped, to use escape routes. On that day, had I looked closely at my telephone conversation with Emily and at the five seconds after I hung up, I could have identified which Paramitas helped in my escape. To begin with, I renounced the impulse—which I felt—to say bad things about our cousin. I was wise enough to know that gossiping would cause Emily pain by detracting from her pleasure in planning the event, which I was determined not to do. I composed myself enough—which took some Energy—to use Right Speech (which was the moral thing to do). I was patient enough to realize the truth: Of course I would go.

Somewhat later—not immediately, because it takes a bit of time for the mind to settle down from a startle—I remembered the many good things I know about that cousin. We grew up together. We have a long list of shared childhood memories. Everything that needed to be done was finished, I knew, when I stopped thinking of "excusable" reasons the cousin might have had for not coming: "The trip is too long." "My health isn't good." "The ticket is expensive." It didn't matter. Any story was acceptable. Coming was not happening. That's all. Forgiving was a great relief, a gift.

RECIPROCAL REACTIONS

My friend Mary and I have shared thirty years of friendship that has included a lot of talk about spiritual commitment. We've agreed on the questions about spiritual practice that we want to ask each other and the people we meet as new friends: "What do you do?" "How do you do it?" "Toward what end?" And the additional question she and I want to ask of ourselves and each other: "Is it working?"

The word *paramita* is from Pali, the language the Buddha spoke, and is usually translated as "perfection." Its derivation is "that which has been completed." Each Paramita quality is understood as an inherent characteristic of the human heart, and a human lifetime—full of both sorrows and joys—is felt to be the most felicitous circumstance for that quality's development. I think of my spiritual life as very much a work in progress, and I use the Paramitas as references for my own path. Am I more generous? More honest? More kind? What works? What doesn't work? What else might I do?

In Massachusetts in 1995, at the Barre Center for Buddhist Studies, I was preparing to teach a daylong retreat organized around the theme of the Ten Perfections. As I had done in similar retreats many times before, I planned to read a Jataka tale, a traditional Buddhist children's story about the Buddha in an earlier incarnation demonstrating great Generosity, or great Patience, or great Determination as a preface to the day. I knew that we would spend most of the day meditating, and I had created meditations—which I'll teach to you at the start of each subsequent chapter of this book—to cultivate each of the Perfections. Each of the meditations strengthens the mind and heart movement that is the parallel internal impulse to each of the Paramitas as actions. In the center's library I read a traditional Paramita text that suggested that practicing each heart quality was both inspired by wisdom and the cause of wisdom. I was delighted. I remembered that at one of my early retreat experiences—just after hearing a lecture about the Buddha's instructions for developing Mindfulness and the value of

Mindfulness—I had written in my journal, "Virtuous behavior supports the ability to pay attention, which then leads to insight, which—in sufficient quantity—becomes wisdom, and wisdom expresses itself, naturally, as compassion." I wrote it—consistent with my earliest adult career as a chemist—as a formula with arrows pointing forward to indicate the sequence of events. It looked like this:

Virtuous behavior→Attention→Insight→Wisdom→Compassion

Then I wondered, "Why not just lead a virtuous life and skip over the mind-training part? Why not just practice compassion and never mind about insight? Maybe if I *behave* as if I have insight, I'll develop some." I thought, "The arrows probably go both ways."

They do. The path of compassion leads to the development of insight. But it doesn't work to say, "Ready, set, go! Be compassionate!" Beginning any practice depends on intention. Intention depends on intuiting—at least a little bit—the suffering inherent in the human condition and the pain we feel, and cause, when we act out of confusion. It also depends on trusting—at least a little bit—in the possibility of a contented, satisfied mind. That intuition and trust are what the Buddha called Wise Understanding. Everyone needs at least a hint of it to start.

So did the Buddha.

According to legend, his royal parents, in response to a soothsayer's claim that the child, Siddhartha Gautama, would grow up to be either a great king or a great spiritual teacher, arranged for him to have an idyllic childhood, free of any distress that might spur his mind into philosophical questioning. Legends also describe how, in his late twenties, as a married man with a young son, he saw—either by going outside the walls of his protected palace under cover of darkness or through the intervention of divine beings who appeared to him as visions—an old person, a sick person, and a corpse. These sights awakened him to the inevitability of loss and grief. A fourth sight, a monk, represented the life of spiritual search for a mind free of suffering, a mind of peace.

The Buddha left home. He meditated. He fasted. He waited. Six years later, when he understood clearly how the mind continues its cycles of suffering by its habits of insatiable wanting, he was free. He knew that peace was possible. Yet he hesitated to teach what he knew, realizing the daunting depth of suffering in the world. He taught anyway *because* of the daunting depth of suffering. Out of compassion.

Introduction: The Paramitas

The Buddha's story is our story.

In the best of circumstances, a loving family, good health, adequate financial resources, and untroubled times are the palace walls that protect our childhoods and early consciousness and allow us to move into our adult lives with confidence. And then, sooner or later, we see what the Buddha saw. We see the truth of change. We begin to understand how fragile life is and how, most surely, we will lose everything that is dear to us. At some point, in some way, we ask ourselves this question: "What is to be done? Is there some way I can do this life with my eyes open and my heart open and still love it? Is there a way not to suffer?"

The pain of that question calls us to attention, just as it did the Buddha. And out of that attention the intention to be free—Wise Intention, the Buddha called it—is born. That intention, whether it starts with insight practice and leads to compassion or begins with compassion and doubles back to insight, supports the whole of Mindfulness practice.

Preparing for the retreat in Barre, reading and studying the Paramita text, and remembering my twenty-year-old speculation about which way the arrows went, I wrote formulas again—ten of them, first as sentences, then as formulas—starting each formula with one of the

Perfections. The first sentence was "Generosity leads to insight into the joy of nongrasping and insight into the truth of suffering." I was pleased that the text had reminded me of my intuition that the arrows must go both ways. So I wrote my formula in a new way:

Virtuous behavior ↔ *Attention* ↔ *Insight* ↔ *Wisdom* ↔ *Compassion*

THE PERIODIC TABLE OF VIRTUE

As further preparation for the Paramita retreat, I drew a chart of my ten formulas—a picture graph of boxes, five across and ten down. I began with Generosity in the top left box—in all of the Paramita lists, Generosity is always the first one listed—and I put Compassion in the bottom right box. I listed the rest of the Paramitas in the first column, the steps in the transformation in the second, third, and fourth columns, and the heart quality that is the full flowering of each Paramita in the last column. In a chemistry class I would have called my chart a flow sheet, a chronicle of all the steps that need to happen to get from A to Z, or, in this case, from Generosity to Compassion. Or, because it looked like a standard chart of the elements of the natural world, I might have called it the Periodic Table of Virtue. This is how it looks:

⌐⌐⌐⌐

Introduction: The Paramitas

REFINING THE QUALITIES OF THE HEART

Particular Expressions of a Compassionate Heart

The practice of:	Develops the habit of:	By:	And is supported by:	And manifests as:
Generosity	Sharing	Experiencing the joy of not feeling needy, the ease of a peaceful mind, the possibility of the end of suffering (the Third Noble Truth)	Realizing that life is inevitably challenging (the First Noble Truth) and discovering the relief that comes with the absence of self-centered preoccupation	Contentment
Morality	Calming	Discovering the joy of practicing Wise Action, Wise Speech, and Wise Livelihood— the relational aspect of the Eightfold Path (the Fourth Noble Truth)	Experiencing the pain of contrition and remorse and the pleasure of making amends (the bliss of blamelessness)	Virtue
Renunciation	Restraining	Realizing that insatiable wanting is suffering (the Second Noble Truth)	Discovering that everything passes, including uncomfortable desires (insight into impermanence)	Temperance

The practice of:	Develops the habit of:	By:	And is supported by:	And manifests as:
Wisdom	Discerning	Understanding that although our minds are continually and inevitably challenged by desires, peace is possible (the First, Second, and Third Noble Truths)	Practicing Wise Effort, Wise Concentration, and Wise Mindfulness, the mind-training aspects of the Eightfold Path, (the Fourth Noble Truth)	Clarity
Energy	Striving	Realizing that there is no time other than now (insight into interdependence)	Focusing on the formidable task of ending suffering, and remembering the possibility of peace (the First and Third Noble Truths)	Indefatigability
Patience	Abiding	Understanding "This will change" and "It cannot be other, yet" (insight into impermanence, and into karma)	Cultivating tranquillity by practicing Wise Concentration (the mind-steadying aspect of the Eightfold Path, the Fourth Noble Truth)	Tolerance

The practice of:	Develops the habit of:	By:	And is supported by:	And manifests as:
Truthfulness	Disclosing	Discovering what is true, and telling the truth in ways that are helpful (practicing Wise Mindfulness and Wise Speech, the mind-clarifying and speech-guiding aspects of the Fourth Noble Truth)	Experiencing the discomforting isolation of guile (separation from self and others) and the ease (and peace) of candor (the Third Noble Truth)	Intimacy
Determination	Persevering	Seeing clearly into the cause of suffering so that the resolve to change habits of mind becomes spontaneous (practicing Wise Understanding and Wise Intention, the mind-energizing aspects of the Fourth Noble Truth)	Validating, through direct experience, the possibility of a peaceful mind (the Third Noble Truth) and consolidating, through repeated experience, the spiritual faculty of faith	Tenacity

The practice of:	Develops the habit of:	By:	And is supported by:	And manifests as:
Lovingkindness	Well-wishing	Celebrating positive qualities in other people, cultivating forgiveness	Remembering that since suffering is universal, everyone is motivated by the desire to be happy (the First Noble Truth)	Kindness
Equanimity	Accepting	Experiencing the happiness of impartiality by paying attention to the whole truth of every moment (practicing Wise Mindfulness, the mind-balancing aspect of the Fourth Noble Truth)	Intuiting and acknowledging that this is a lawful cosmos, just and comforting in its dependability; understanding karma, cause and effect, and interdependence	Compassion

At the retreat, I taught with the chart in front of me as my only text. I began the first meditation session by saying, "Everything depends on paying attention. We'll work with each Paramita individually, but let's first establish a foundation of Mindfulness—balanced, clear, moment-to-moment attention. We could choose anything that's happening right now to pay attention to, but

~~~~

let's use the experience of breathing. Breath is an imme-
diate, reliable connection to the present moment. It's always happening. And it's ordinary, predictable, and
repetitive. Limiting your attention to just the breath
calms the mind down. You don't need to *do* anything at
all. Think of it as a kindness to your mind, like a
Sabbath."

I invited people to meditate in that way for several
minutes, and you might like to do that also, right now,
before continuing to read. Think of it as the preparation
for the directed-attention practice of cultivating the
specific energies of the Paramitas. This is plain, alert,
resting-in-the-moment practice. Just close your eyes and
feel the sensations of your breath coming in and out in
its own natural rhythm. When you feel relaxed but still
alert, open your eyes and continue.

I always begin to teach the Paramitas by talking
about Generosity. I say that the Buddha recommended
we start with Generosity because we all have *something*
we could give away. At the retreat, I began the instructions as people were still sitting quietly, mindfully attentive to their breathing. I said, "Now, as a Generosity
meditation, see if you can give away any discursive dialogue—what you'll do later, what you did yesterday.
You don't need those thoughts now.

"If they're important, they'll come back later. Enjoy the feeling of your mind relaxing, not needing anything other than this moment of awareness and of your body breathing naturally." You might try that too, if you'd like, right now. Just for a minute or two. If you do, you'll notice that your mind will wake up a little bit because now you are paying attention more carefully to what's happening, and actively choosing the breath over everything else. And actively giving away. Not-needing is a very pleasant feeling. See if you can feel that, and then read on.

As we sat, I thought of Generosity stories that I knew, and after the meditation period, I told them. The whole day passed that way as we practiced one Paramita after the other. I followed my chart. I gave meditation instructions that developed the particular mind habit that supported each of the Paramitas. I told stories appropriate to each particular quality of heart. And I realized with great delight that the "flow sheet" I'd created—designating specific insights as the conditioning factors for each of the Paramitas—was carrying me along from line to line, box to box, Paramita to Paramita, without my needing to preplan. I thought, "This chart will tell me what to say. I can relax!"

At the end of that day in Barre, I made notes to myself on my chart of the particular stories I had told as examples of each Paramita, and for a while afterward I carried that very chart with me as a reminder. Now I teach with an unmarked chart, because the stories I tell change all the time as the most recent Determination story or Truthfulness story replaces—by natural self-selection—the one I used to tell. It's better that way. I *do* try to remember to take my chart with me when I travel to teach. I like having it in front of me, and I always enjoy having the boxes fill with stories as the conclusion—"Virtue is both the cause of happiness and the expression of happiness"—builds throughout the day. Sometimes I forget the chart, or I give it away to someone who likes it enough to ask for it.

The truth is, having a chart is optional. Even the order of the list of Paramitas—which is traditional—is arbitrary. Starting anywhere ends everywhere. It's not possible to cultivate any single Paramita without all of the others developing. They depend on each other. Each is a permutation and combination of all the others, each quality revealing all of the others, like a hologram. The ten Paramitas together are the one path to goodness and kindness. Each particular quality is an entryway into that path, and it's likely that whatever quality is our strongest becomes the support for the development of all of the others. Some people's nervous systems seem by temperament geared for Patience. Some people do Renunciation easily. Others naturally have plenty of Energy. It's inspiring to know that the development of any one Paramita enhances all of the others, because it means that we can begin, with confidence, wherever we are.

Let's start.

CHAPTER ONE

Generosity

//////////////////////////

Generosity brings happiness at every stage of its expression.
We experience joy in forming the intention to be generous.
We experience joy in the actual act of giving something.
And we experience joy in remembering the fact that we have
given.
—THE BUDDHA

GENEROSITY

The practice of:	Develops the habit of:	By:	And is supported by:	And manifests as:
Generosity	Sharing	Experiencing the joy of not feeling needy, the ease of a peaceful mind, the possibility of the end of suffering (the Third Noble Truth)	Realizing that life is inevitably challenging (the First Noble Truth) and discovering the relief that comes with the absence of self-centered preoccupation	Contentment

I say this chart to myself this way: If I intend to perfect my capacity for Generosity, I need to be alert for every opportunity that presents itself in which I can share. The sharing itself, the generous act, will become the habit by means of which I can experience directly the joy of not feeling needy, the ease of a peaceful mind. And I'll be inspired to cultivate that habit of sharing by recognizing that my life (and everyone else's too) is challenged, and that comforting and being comforted are pleasures. When I feel I have enough, I am content.

GENEROSITY MEDITATION

I have a framed Nicole Hollander *Sylvia* cartoon on the wall in my kitchen. Sylvia is typing a list of "responses you hope to have the occasion to say." Everyone always laughs at "Yes, it is unusual to have won an Olympic medal and the Nobel peace prize *and* could you bring me leather pants in a size two?" They laugh at Sylvia's answer to the question "Ma, do you want anything from the store?" "Just get me two of everything." And they chuckle, as I always do, when they read the response that tops Sylvia's typed list: "No, thanks. I have everything I need."

The best thing about generosity is enjoying the feeling of not-needing. It's a great freedom. So stop. You don't *need* to go on right now. The whole book will wait. Smile. Take a long breath in and out. In whatever position you are—sitting up or lying down—make yourself comfortable. In a minute, when you finish reading the instructions, you'll close your eyes. But now, as you read, notice that you can feel your body, especially now that I've directed your attention to it, even as you read.

You'll notice that your body, in a regular pattern, fills with breath as air comes into it and then eases back down as the breath goes out. No one *needs* to do anything. Breathing happens all by itself, and awareness happens all by itself. In the next several minutes, after you've closed your eyes, you will be able to let your awareness rest just in this sensation. Think of it as a gift to yourself, a sabbatical. To support your gift, give away any thought that arises in your mind that might captivate or distract your attention. Even if it seems important, you don't need it. If it's important, it will come back later. Let it go. Open your hands, whether they are on your lap or alongside you, into a relaxed shape, a shape that shows you have enough. Now close your eyes, relax, and practice this Generosity meditation for as long as you like.

RESOUNDING GENEROSITY

My friend and teaching colleague James Baraz tells the story of how he still experiences the pleasure that he felt thirty years ago sharing a piece of cake with three of his friends. I think I've heard the story at least two dozen times, and I still love hearing it. He tells it at retreats, as part of a Dharma talk (a lecture on what the Buddha taught), and seldom varies a single word of it. I know all the details—how, while he was a meditator at a silent retreat washing pots as his afternoon work assignment, one of the cooks offered him a piece of cheesecake, a rare treat that had not been part of the lunch for the retreatants. He describes his delight. Then he explains that in those days people washed their own dishes and cups and set them on shelves along the wall to await the next meal. James knew which dishes belonged to his friends. He describes cutting his cake into four pieces, eating one piece himself, and putting the three other pieces on his friends' dishes. By the time James arrives at the point in the story where he tells about the looks of pleasure and surprise on his friends' faces as they arrived for the evening meal and found the cake in their dishes, and how he felt seeing them, he is clearly reliving the happiness of that moment. I feel it sitting next to him. I hear it in his voice. I think everyone else in the room does too. The echo of that piece of cheesecake is still reverberating.

The particulars of Generosity stories vary, of course, but certain elements are present in all of them. Formal translations of traditional Buddhist texts say, "The proximal cause for the arising of generosity is realizing that something can be relinquished." This means that acts of

Generosity are preceded by the awareness "I have this, and I can give it away. I don't *need* to keep it." What also has to be present is the awareness of having something that might be useful, pleasant, or comforting to other people, as well as a sense of other people's needs.

Louise M. Davies was the principal donor for the building of the very beautiful symphony hall in San Francisco. It's named for her. A newspaper story, just after the building was inaugurated, quoted her response to an interviewer's question: "Why did you give this gift of six million dollars?"

She was said to have replied, "Because I had it."

I thought her answer was wonderful. It was so uncomplicated. It was stating the obvious. Of *course* she had it. Otherwise she couldn't have given it. And although she could have offered an opinion ("San Francisco needs a symphony hall with modern acoustics") or a personal reflection ("I've always loved music. It's important to me"), she didn't do that either. She just said, "I had it." So simple.

Sitting in Davies Hall enjoying a performance, I've often thought, "She could have had it and *not* given it." Not feeling needy is what *allows* generosity to happen, but it doesn't obligate it to happen. The impulse to *do* something has to be present. Recognizing the possibility of creating delight or of alleviating suffering are both sources of that impulse. Both are responses to people other than ourselves. Both provide pleasure.

In 1990 James and I traveled to India with some of our friends to visit the venerable Advaita teacher Sri H. W. L. Poonja in Lucknow. Every day for three weeks we traveled (in three-wheel taxis, then by pedal rickshaw, then on foot) to arrive in time for morning *darshan* (teachings) at his home. We sat with perhaps twenty other students from all over the world, squeezed in close to each other on the floor of the small living room. Poonja-ji (the *-ji* is an affectionate honorific title for a teacher) sat on a raised platform in the front of the room. For three hours he told stories, laughed, and included each of us, one by one, in dialogue. We all loved it. On the last day he agreed to see James and me in a private interview.

"What do you teach?" he asked.

"We teach Mindfulness and Lovingkindness meditation," James replied, "and we especially emphasize Generosity."

"There is no such thing as Generosity," Poonja-ji said. James and I exchanged glances that said, "Uh-oh! Have we just started this interview and already done it wrong?"

"No such thing at all," Poonja-ji repeated. "There is only the awareness of need and the natural impulse of the heart to address it. If you are hungry and your hand puts food in your mouth, you don't think of the hand as generous, do you? If people in front of you are hungry and you feed them, it's the same, isn't it?"

James and I talked afterward. "Maybe he's right," I said. "Let's think this through. If in the spring, as I am putting away my winter clothes, I think, 'I didn't wear this at all. I'll give it to the Salvation Army,' maybe that *isn't* Generosity. Maybe it's just closet cleaning. Maybe Generosity is happening when I'm thinking, 'I *did* wear this a few times. It is still stylish. I like it. I could save it and wear it sometime, or I could give it to the Salvation Army,' and then *finally* decide, 'I'll give it away.' Maybe *that's* Generosity." I looked at James. "Isn't that Generosity?"

"Maybe," James said, "it's a moment of realizing that not-needing has won out over needing."

"Or," I said, "that someone else's needing has won out over my needing."

I know it works that way for me. When I am not confused or frightened, I'm able to respond to needs beyond my own. I think that's true for everyone. When we are personally at ease, the pain of other people—even people we don't know—touches us, and we are moved to end it. Responding feels more comfortable than *not* responding. And I think that when people say "Thank you" in response to a kindness we've offered them, we say "It's my pleasure" because it *is*.

James and I ended our conversation by agreeing, "Maybe there is no such thing as someone who is generous. Maybe there are only causes and conditions for relinquishing and receiving. But there *is* Generosity."

Generosity arises in response to the awareness of particular beneficiaries and particular needs. When we deliver a gift personally, we get to have the pleasure of seeing the response. When we contribute to a cause—preserving national parks, or ensuring voting rights, or funding cancer research—we imagine how our gift will be received. I think Louise Davies must have been very pleased by the thought that thousands and thousands of people—including people like myself—would enjoy the music if she gave the gift that would build the hall.

Also, she had it.

ONE ROBE, ONE BOWL

At Spirit Rock Meditation Center there is a basket on the table in the entrance foyer of the Community

Meditation Hall with a card that says DANA on it. When newcomers arrive for a class, they probably figure out—especially if they are familiar with collection plates at churches—that the people stopping to put money into the basket are making some gesture of voluntary support. *Dana* is the Pali word for "generosity," and at Spirit Rock we teach it as a practice.

My ability to be generous varies—as does everyone's—with how comfortable I feel. Generosity depends on not feeling needy. I'd learned, before my first formal Mindfulness retreat, that the money I would be asked to pay for the retreat would be the cost of room and board at the retreat center and that, in keeping with the tradition in Asia, there was no established fee for the teachings. I liked the explanation given for the tradition: "Since these teachings are priceless, it's not possible to charge for them." I knew that retreatants, eager to express their gratitude and also aware that the teachers needed to support themselves, left gifts of money at the end of retreats.

I finished that retreat so inspired and happy about the possibility of freedom from suffering and so hopeful that practice might provide that for me that I thought, "This *is* priceless. I should give everything I have." Then I thought, "That can't be right. It doesn't make sense. I'm a householder. I have a family to care for." In the end, I made my *dana* offering a practice, as I do now, of deciding, given my current circumstances, on a responsible expression of my gratitude. The gift decision, though, was not what mattered. What mattered was that in the moment of impulsive, generous thought, I absolutely knew that the only thing I *needed* was freedom.

Not long after that, still in the early years of my practice, a group of Burmese monks were guest teachers for a week at a retreat at which I was a student in southern California. They were housed in one of the cottages at the edge of the retreat center. One morning after breakfast, the retreat manager announced, "The monks are leaving this morning. If you want to, you can stand outside their cottage as a gesture of respect as they leave."

I stood silently with the other retreatants and watched the monks walk out single file from their cottage, each one carrying his begging bowl in a string bag. I realized that whatever they were wearing, whatever they were carrying, and whatever was in the two suitcases on top of the minibus they were traveling in constituted all of their worldly goods. Watching the monks seemed to me a visual representation of the truth that not-needing—not needing more, not needing other—is the end of suffering. I thought, "They have everything they need."

At home these days, I keep a copy of a small book of poetry by the Zen monk Ryokan, *One Robe, One Bowl,* not on the bookshelf but someplace where I see it often—on the kitchen counter, or propped up on the piano next to the music. The title reminds me of the image of the monks. When my mind becomes cluttered, and therefore tense, with desires—with things I think I need or ways in which I think things need to be in order for me to be happy—I remember that the clutter itself is the cause of my suffering, and I think, "What is it that I *really* need?" When I see clearly enough, I can be generous toward myself. I can give away the clutter.

REALLY GREAT GENEROSITY

I've heard people use the expression "generous to a fault," as if it were possible to be *too* generous, that great Generosity would somehow be depriving oneself. I think the opposite is true. Being able to give freely means not being so absorbed in one's own needs that it becomes impossible to look past them at who else is in the world and what *they* need. Not being absorbed in one's own needs is—even before any generous act happens—a relief.

The Buddha taught that suffering is the extra pain in the mind that happens when we feel an anguished imperative to have things be different from how they are. We see it most clearly when our personal situation is painful and we want very much for it to change. It's the wanting very much that hurts so badly, the feeling of "I need this desperately," that paralyzes the mind. The "I" who wants so much feels isolated. Alone.

Generous acts are a relief because they connect. They are always in relationship. They can't be isolating. And generous acts don't require some *thing* to give away. I understand the Buddha's statement "We all have something we could give away" as including—in addition to material possessions—companionship, comfort, encouragement, and care. I think about realizing how the act of giving wholeheartedly—whatever one has to give—not only does not diminish one's resources, but can be lifesaving to both the receiver and the giver of the gift.

My next-door neighbor, Jesse, died at home, of colon cancer, twenty-five years ago. When I visited him just days before he died, he explained, pointing to the bottles and hypodermic needles arranged on his bedside table, that because he was a physician, he was in charge of his own pain control.

"This is morphine," he said, "and I give it to myself when the pain gets too terrible." He paused and looked at me as if considering whether or not to go on. "Sometimes," he said, "I think about killing myself. I could, you know. It would be easy. I could just take too much morphine. Each time I get ready to do it, though, I think of someone else I need to tell something to. I have a friend in Atlanta with a new business, and I have some good ideas for him. And my nephew in L.A. has marriage problems. I think I could help him. Sometimes I can't think of one more thing I need to do, but then I think I *might*. So I don't do it."

I recall that as Jesse and I visited, I was thinking about how kind he was to be remembering his friends and their needs in the last days of his own life. I still remember him as kind, of course, but now I also think Jesse was very lucky. What a relief it must have been for him to fill his mind with ideas about what he could *do* rather than with sad stories about dying. I don't think that Jesse figured out, "The wise thing for me to do so that I *feel* alive as long as I *am* alive is to connect." I think he just did the wise thing naturally. That's why I think he was lucky.

And I marvel at what the mind can do naturally, even

in pain, even foggy with morphine. Perhaps it's the awareness "I'm going to die later today, or tomorrow" that wakes up the mind's ability to pay attention. Maybe Generosity, really *great* Generosity, is the expression of the deeply felt recognition that I become part of your life when I give you something of mine and you become part of my life when you accept it. In fact, underneath this world full of people who appear to be separate, living and dying individually, we are all part of life unfolding. *That's* the insight that frees us from the endless burden of worrying about ourselves: There is just us to look after.

My friend Paul was driving across the United States from San Francisco to Massachusetts and a new job when he got the news that the National Bone Marrow Registry was trying to locate him. Several months earlier, having met someone whose life had been saved by a bone marrow transplant and learning that people with no kinship relationship at all can be a compatible match for each other, Paul had donated a sample of his blood for testing. When he phoned the registry from western Kansas, he was told that his sample matched a person in New York City, acutely ill and needing a transplant. He then phoned his new employers to postpone his arrival for three days, drove to New York, checked into the hospital, and spent three days there—one day for preparation for the surgery, one day for the bone marrow transplant, and one day recuperating—and then finished his drive to Massachusetts.

Paul told me the story of the transplant when we first met, almost a year later. He said that he knew that "his recipient" was still living, and that if both parties want to meet, one year after a successful transplant each can learn who the other person is.

"I don't want to know," Paul said. "I am having such a good time *not* knowing. I pass people in supermarkets and I think, 'Maybe *that's* my person.' Or I think about the man sitting next to me on a bus, or the young girl looking out the window of the plane whom I see just in passing on my way to the back of the plane, and I think, 'Maybe *that's* my person.' Since I don't know for sure, I can imagine that everyone is my person. It's much better this way."

THIS *IS* THE REAL WORLD:
EVERYDAY GENEROSITY PRACTICE

One of the very first stories I heard about meditation described a hermit emerging from his cave after years of meditation, having achieved a mind of perfect calm and peace. He visits the local marketplace. Someone accidentally jostles him. He hits back. When I heard the story, I laughed. But I got the point. A mind of perfect calm and peace that lasts only as far as the exit of the cave is not the goal of practice. It needs to get out the door.

At the end of retreats, people often ask me, "How can I take this practice back into the real world?" I always respond, "This *is* the real world." I acknowledge that a retreat center is a unique place in the world, where we agree to live in a special form—like hermits—meditating many hours every day, not reading, not writing, and not talking to each other. I say as well that it's a wonderful, functional form, one in which the silence and the simplicity of the schedule support the mind's natural ability to pay attention. "But," I say, "it's just a form. It's not the practice. The practice is keeping your mind clear and your heart loving."

We have the same minds and hearts in retreat centers, meditation classes, churches, and synagogues as we have in supermarkets. We practice in quiet, contemplative surroundings when we can in order to have our minds clear and our hearts loving all the rest of the time. Paying attention is a completely portable practice. You take it with you wherever you go.

Paramita practice is equally portable. We can practice each of the Perfections contemplatively, internally developing and strengthening the particular habits and insights that support them. And we can practice each of them by deciding to behave in the world in ways that firm up the natural inclination of our hearts to goodness. Maybe it's like belonging to two gyms, the Gym of the *Zafu* (meditation cushion) and the Gym of the Marketplace. Since they are mutually supporting venues for practice, each of the chapters of this book will be framed by "inner" and "outer" exercises. Here is the first everyday, real-world exercise.

This Generosity practice was the idea of several members of the Wednesday morning class at Spirit Rock Meditation Center, who decided—although someone said, laughing, "I feel like a Girl Scout"—to commit to doing five unscheduled acts of Generosity every day. For the duration of the experiment, they reported back to the group each week. Mostly they gave time. "I let the person behind me in the bank have my place." "I passed up a parking space because I could see the person behind me wanted it." We decided that we wouldn't count church dues, symphony support, or any other gifts that we give as a matter of course and that don't require daily attention. We were testing the hypothesis that the joy of generosity would be heightened if *looking* for the opportunity to give something to someone, *planning* to do it, *doing* it, and *seeing* the response were all present. The people in the class said it was exciting—like a treasure hunt with a time limit—and that it was difficult. It required a lot of paying attention to find five opportunities every day. They loved it.

Perhaps you'll try it. Here's a hint: Find a friend who'll agree to do it with you and tell each other, often, how you're doing. Paying attention to the question "Who is around me that I can do something for?" connects us to the world. Talking with friends about our goodness connects us more deeply to each other.

CHAPTER TWO

Morality

✓✓✓✓✓✓✓✓✓✓✓✓✓✓✓✓✓✓✓✓

A compassionate great ape, a prior incarnation of the Buddha, rescued a man who had fallen into a deep pit in the forest, carrying him to the top on his back. Exhausted, the ape said, "I need to sleep so I'll have the strength to help you find the way out of the forest. You watch over me." As he slept, the man, overcome by hunger, thought, "I need to kill this ape and eat him." He picked up a huge boulder and threw it—with all his might—on the sleeping ape. The ape awoke, startled. His eyes filled with tears. "You poor man," he said. "Now you will never be happy."
—A Jataka Tale

MORALITY

The practice of:	Develops the habit of:	By:	And is supported by:	And manifests as:
Morality	Calming	Discovering the joy of practicing Wise Action, Wise Speech, and Wise Livelihood— the relational aspects of the Eightfold Path (the Fourth Noble Truth)	Experiencing the pain of contrition and remorse and the pleasure of making amends (the bliss of blamelessness)	Virtue

If I intend to perfect my Morality, I'll need to be sure I stay calm enough to ensure that I don't do anything heedlessly. My commitment to the Buddha's specific guidelines for Wise Action, Wise Livelihood, and Wise Speech—the parts of the Eightfold Path (Fourth Noble Truth) most directly governing my behavior in the world—acts as a fail-safe mechanism to keep my mind, inflamed by some passion, from saying, "Go for it. Just

〰〰〰

this one time." That commitment stays strong if I acknowledge the pain I feel when I cause suffering, how glad I am to repair injuries, how pleasant it is to feel that there is no one toward whom and nothing about which I feel guilty. The Buddha called that good feeling the bliss of blamelessness.

MORALITY MEDITATION

The practice of Morality habituates the mind to calm. When the mind is calm, there is generally enough composure in it to allow for reflection and enough balance to stay comfortable. A comfortable mind is unlikely to generate unskillful behavior because it doesn't need to leap, impulsively, after desires. It thinks before it acts.

The *Foundations of Mindfulness,* the Buddha's instruction sermon for the practice of Mindfulness, begins with the instruction to be in a quiet place, to sit still, and to direct attention to the breath. Practitioners are then asked to notice the quality of the breaths—some short, some long—as they naturally arise, and are invited to discover that the careful attention they bring to the breaths calms the body. The calm itself then becomes the focus of attention, and the meditator is instructed to reflect with each breath, "As I breathe in, I am calmed," and "As I breathe out, I am calmed."

When I do this exercise, I often make my inhalations and exhalations just a wee bit longer than they might be on their own, at least for the first few minutes. Extending each breath just slightly keeps me paying attention and reminds me of my intention to establish calm. I do one more thing. I use the Buddha's instructions for inhaling and say, "Breathing in, I calm my body." And I use the contemporary Vietnamese teacher Thich Nhat Hanh's instruction for exhaling and say, "Breathing out, I smile."

Now you try it. "Breathing in, I calm my body. Breathing out, I smile." Close your eyes. Sit as long as you like.

THE RIGHT SPEECH KOAN OF MAX'S CAFÉ

"What is the sound of one hand clapping?" is not a normal question—since one hand, by definition, cannot clap—so it cannot have a normal answer. It's probably the most well known example of a koan, an enigmatic word or situation that practitioners in the Rinzai Zen tradition muse over as part of their meditation practice to coax the mind into more subtle levels of understanding. The musing—turning the question over and over in the mind—is more important than arriving at the right answer. Students in that tradition are assigned their koans individually, by their teacher, following an established pattern. I was given a koan, quite by accident, in the ladies' room of Max's Café in Corte Madera, California. It was a ten-second transmission, but it engaged my attention for some weeks and kept unfolding . . . perhaps even now, in this writing.

I was out at Max's for a late supper with my friend Martha, and as I was washing my hands at the sink in the ladies' room, I looked up and saw in the mirror the reflection of a woman standing at the next sink who had both her hands behind her head, apparently working at undoing whatever clip or tie was holding her blond hair pulled back into a tight bun. As I watched, she shook her head, and a giant mane of wavy, Farrah Fawcett hair poofed out around her head and shoulders.

"Oh!" I said, sincerely delighted by her remarkable transformation. "You have such *beautiful* hair! I've always admired that kind of hair."

The young woman seemed startled. She turned to me, said, "Well, if it makes you feel any better, I'm very unhappy," and left the ladies' room.

I stood there, at first surprised, and then miffed.

"Hmpf!" I thought. "Do I look like the type of person who would feel better knowing that she is unhappy?" I could feel my back straighten with indignation, and my mind began to construct a "Can you *imagine* what happened in the ladies' room?" story for Martha.

Back at my table, I told Martha my story, somewhat dramatically, and Martha, predictably, became vicariously miffed on my behalf. "What bad manners!" she said. "Not nice at all!"

Suddenly I became aware that I had, in a misguided attempt to soothe my own hurt feelings, ruined Martha's good mood and cast aspersions on a young woman whose situation I knew nothing about. Two mistakes—three, counting the hair remark—in two minutes.

"Wait a minute, Martha," I said. "I'm just now realizing that I have *no* idea at all about the mind state into which I made that apparently ill-timed, albeit good-spirited, remark. No idea at all. I don't know if five minutes before we met at the sinks, her partner of ten years said, 'I don't love you anymore' or whether she lost her job today, or if she just had a glass of wine after twelve years of sobriety. All I know is that I intruded."

I looked around Max's hoping to locate the young, beautiful, unhappy woman. I thought about—and dismissed as awkward—apologizing for startling her. I didn't see her anywhere.

"I need to make some internal amends," I told Martha. "Let's do some *metta* [Lovingkindness] prayers for her. 'Wherever you are, and whatever your pain, may your suffering be over. May your mind be at ease.'"

"How about for you too?" Martha said. "May you also be at ease."

"Yes," I agreed, "for me too."

In the days and weeks that followed—because the situation kept turning itself over in my mind—I told that story to all the classes I taught. I taught it as a Morality reflection and presented it as a koan on Right Speech: "When is Right Speech Wrong Speech?" The Buddha's guideline for Right Speech is that it be both truthful *and* helpful. When it is not absolutely clear that both criteria have been met, the guidelines suggest maintaining Noble Silence.

The Max's Café conversation inspired a lot of enthusiastic commentary, and in the end, the prevailing opinion was definitely *not* in favor of not talking to strangers in public places, refraining from telling people they are pretty, or inhibiting any other well-intended spontaneity. The general conclusion was "You never can really know, however well-intentioned you are, how your act will fall. If it comes out less helpful than you had hoped, you make amends. If you can't, you make internal amends—you pray. You didn't *know* it wasn't going to turn out well." Someone said, "It's not a Right Speech koan, it's a Right Intention koan."

After I thought the story had run its entire teaching course, my friend Jonathan added one more piece. He said, "I think you've left something out. You don't know if three months from now that very woman, standing in front of a mirror, brushing her hair, looking at herself, might find herself thinking, 'You know, I have really nice hair. I have *beautiful* hair. A person I didn't know at all told me that in a ladies' room somewhere.' Maybe at that time it will be something she can feel good about, something that will make her feel happy. Perhaps the fact that you put that idea out into the universe will ultimately turn out to be helpful to her. You don't know that it won't turn out well."

Jonathan was right. I *don't* know. I form opinions—I think we all do—extrapolating from current data and imagining that I know, for sure, how things will turn out. If I pay attention to—in fact, if I turn over and over again in my mind—the ways in which I mistake views for truths, the Max's story becomes a Right Wisdom koan.

A Right Speech koan? A Right Intention koan? A Right Wisdom koan? All of the above? A Right Everything koan? "When is everything everything?" *That's* a good koan.

MAKING AND MENDING MISTAKES

In a Morality sermon preached for his son called Advice for Rahula, the Buddha said that there are three times that a person should consider the consequences of any action: before, during, and after. "One should reflect thus," he said. "'Is what I am about to do . . .' or 'Is what I am currently doing . . .' or 'Is what I just did . . . for my own well-being *and* for the benefit of all others?'" I was especially impressed with this teaching when I first learned it because it was accompanied by the reminder that *every* action—even the decision *not* to act—creates results that endure, in an eternal cause-and-effect ripple, forever. I took equally to heart the parallel teaching that it is possible—indeed, imperative—to change course, or to repair an action, whenever it is a mistake.

I am relieved when I recognize in advance of doing something that my intention is unkind. I think, "Whew! Narrow escape! No one knows about this but me. Now I won't do it." I am also relieved, although often chagrined, to find myself in mid-foolishness. I stop and say to whoever is involved, "I'm sorry. I'm in the middle of making a mistake. I'll start again. Please forgive me." I feel unhappy when I discover I have acted in ways that cause pain. I make whatever amends I can. I say, "I'm sorry. I made a mistake. Please forgive me." I've discovered that the relief I feel when my contrition is heartfelt and my amends and apology are accepted restores my happiness. It also inspires my zeal for paying attention so that I get it right the first time. I also know that if I don't get it right the first time, my heart remembers it forever, very often long after my conscious mind forgets, and long after amends are possible.

My friend Susan drove me from Woodstock, New York, where I had led a Mindfulness retreat, to Boston, where I was scheduled to teach a daylong seminar on the Perfections. I felt good about how I'd taught in Woodstock, and I was thrilled by the October leaf display on the Taconic Parkway, so my mind was especially relaxed and alert. Perhaps that's why the sweeping view of the Hudson River as we crossed the Kingston-Rhinecliff Bridge dislodged a memory of an unkindness I had done on a Hudson River Day Line Cruise to Bear Mountain in the spring of 1950. As unkindnesses go, it seemed small. "Featherweight," I thought when it first came to mind. But as I thought about how long it had taken for that memory to surface and how bad I felt about it, I began to imagine a huge pile of similar feathers under which this particular one had been hidden. I remembered that the answer to the children's riddle "How much does a ton of feathers weigh?" is "One ton."

"Susan," I said, "I have a confession to make. I hurt a young boy's feelings once, long ago, on this river. We were high school students, violin players in an orchestra that celebrated the end of the academic year with a picnic at Bear Mountain State Park. He had asked me to be his date for that day. I had agreed, although secretly I was embarrassed by how shy and awkward he was. Probably," I added with clarity that arose as I spoke, "I felt embarrassed about how shy and awkward *I* was. I don't remember much of the day," I went on, "but I clearly recall walking down the length of the deck of the Day Liner looking for a bathroom, and passing a troop of Eagle Scouts from Des Moines on holiday in New York who called out flirting remarks to me. I flirted back. I liked the Scout uniforms. I thought they were cute. Everyone smoked cigarettes. I thought that was sophisticated. I spent hours with them, smoking cigarettes, laughing at their jokes, practicing what I thought was chic banter. That was it," I said. "Nothing more complicated happened. Now I remember a sad-faced boy taking me home at the end of the day. I wish I could make amends."

"Do you remember his name?" Susan asked.

"Oh yes, I do," I said, "but it's the kind of name that makes me sure that there are at least ten sixty-five-year-old men in every major East Coast metropolis with that same name. How would I find the very one?"

"You could try the Internet," Susan suggested.

"No, I can't," I said. "What would I say? 'If you are the Marvin Goldstein I humiliated fifty years ago on an orchestra boat trip to Bear Mountain, I feel bad. Please forgive me'?" Maybe *the* Marvin Goldstein I humiliated will read it and feel *publicly* humiliated. Maybe *other* Marvin Goldsteins who were, in other circumstances, humiliated will have their personal pain revived. Maybe the Marvin Goldstein I *think* I humiliated hadn't noticed my behavior and my memory of his sad face is incorrect. None of those solutions is any good, anyway," I said. "It would be a confession that I would be making for *my* benefit, so that I could be forgiven. Not for *his* benefit. That's the thing about confessing," I said. "It gets things off our chest—but if it's not useful news for the other person, and especially if it's hurtful news, it makes things worse. When the circumstances aren't right, or the time isn't right, to include the other person in the amends, we need to do them in our own heart."

We drove for a while quietly. "What are you thinking about?" Susan asked.

"I'm sending prayers of good wishes to Marvin Goldstein," I said, "wherever he is. It's the best I can do at this point. I hope he is well. And I'm thinking about what other feathers of painful memories I've got still hidden away. I'm hoping they don't all dump themselves into my mind at the same time, but a gradual moral inventory wouldn't be so bad. When I feel a cycle complete itself—remembering, remorse, contrition, genuine well-wishing, and finally forgiving myself—I feel much lighter."

The next day I told that story when I taught in Boston. I used it as an illustration, explaining how the dedication to Morality comes from realizing, deeply, how bad we feel when we discover that we've hurt someone and how long that bad feeling can stay hidden in our minds. I said, "If I think about how my unkindness might have affected the boy I was with—already shy and awkward before that experience—and if I think about what else might be hidden, I am inspired, more than ever, to pay attention."

"It was just one afternoon," someone said, "a long

time ago. Maybe it wasn't that important to him. Maybe it didn't matter."

"And anyway," someone else said, "you don't think you can be perfect, do you?"

"No," I said. "I'm sure I *can't* be perfect. I pay attention so I won't be worse. And," I added, "I think *everything* matters."

I reminded people of the description of how a butterfly flapping its wings in Vermont becomes one of the causes—not the *only* cause, of course, but one of them—of a typhoon sweeping by the coast of Indonesia six months later. The butterfly flapping is a neutral cause, nonvolitional, just as a typhoon is an impersonal, natural event, making landfall and causing destruction by circumstance of wind and weather. It is thoughtless.

I said that treating a shy and awkward young man casually, in a way that might make him feel ashamed, is also thoughtless. Butterflies and typhoons, though, are nonvolitional. What people do *is* volitional. I said I felt sorry about having been thoughtless and hoped it had been a small matter. "Still," I said, "when I saw the Hudson yesterday and remembered that day long ago, I did think, 'Just as a butterfly flaps its wings . . .' and 'Just as a shy boy musters up the courage to ask a girl he fancies out as his date . . .'"

Several people in the class raised their hands to speak.

"Last week a homeless person asked me for money for a bus ticket to Worcester, and I only gave him three dollars. I thought he was conning me. All week long I've been troubled about it. I wish I'd given him enough for a ticket."

"Twenty-three years ago I told my mother a lie and she *knew* it was a lie. Now she has Alzheimer's and won't understand me if I explain it."

"My sister-in-law found out I'd said something mean about her to my brother. She hasn't talked to me for four years. I shouldn't have said it. And I should have apologized more. I apologized once, but she was still hurt, so I got mad at her back. I should have kept apologizing. Now there is so much bad feeling in the family, I don't know if we can fix it. I feel terrible. It was my fault."

The stories continued for a long time. Morality seems close to our hearts, and moral inventory clearly has no statute of limitations. As they listened to each other, people were reminded of something they wanted to tell. And as I listened, I realized that telling others about mistakes we have made, things we regret having done, puts us in touch with the goodness in ourselves, the part of us that wishes we had done it differently.

Someone said, "This is a surprise. I thought, as we all started to speak, that this would be demoralizing, that we'd drag each other down. But I feel glad. And relieved."

REFUGES AND PRECEPTS

All over the world, people whose spiritual practice is inspired by the Buddha's teaching ally themselves to their own community and to the lineage community of Buddhists by reciting formal Refuge vows:

I take refuge in the Buddha.
I take refuge in the Dharma (the Buddha's teachings).
I take refuge in the *Sangha*
(the community of practitioners).

And they remind themselves of the moral guidelines for practitioners by reciting the Five Precepts:

I vow to abstain from harming living beings.
I vow to abstain from taking what is not freely given.
I vow to abstain from sexual misconduct.
I vow to abstain from incorrect speech.
I vow to abstain from intoxicants that lead
to heedlessness.

At Spirit Rock Meditation Center we recite Refuges and Precepts as group practice at the beginning of all retreats. We usually chant the Precepts in Pali, the language of the Buddha, to honor the lineage of Buddhist teachers through whom the practice of Mindfulness has been preserved. We recite them a second time in English.

I teach Refuges and Precepts as Morality practice, and I explain them this way: When I say, "I take refuge in the Buddha," I remember that the Buddha, a human being just as I am, was able to understand the causes of suffering and the end of suffering well enough to feel himself free, and I am inspired in my own practice. "I take refuge in the Dharma" is my expression of trust that the practice program of the Eightfold Path is valid, that it is working to support the inclination of my heart toward kindness. And "I take refuge in the *Sangha*" connects me to "fellow Dharma-farers" (Buddhist practitioners) and to everyone else whose practice life supports mine.

The first precept, "I vow to abstain from harming living beings," seems to me the summary of all the rest. The next three precepts are reminders of specific ways in which, if we don't pay attention, we might harm. Blinded by lust, anger, or fear, we might steal, use our sexuality abusively, or speak destructively. I think of the fifth precept, dedication to sobriety of mind, as the practice intention that completes the first Precept vow: Vowing to abstain from harming living beings, I resolve to pay attention so that I do not become confused.

When I first began teaching, I led people in reciting Refuges and Precepts as the obligatory form for opening a retreat, or at the beginning of daylong classes, but I felt hesitant about it and rarely mentioned them apart from those times. I thought that saying "Now let's take the Precepts . . ." implied that we didn't all live morally in our regular lives, or that we would behave differently when the day or the retreat was over. I would say, "Of course we already live this way in our regular lives. We say the Precepts here to remind each other of what we value. It's just a form."

Now I do it differently. I say, "This is an *amazing* form. As we recite these Precepts together now, I hope you will feel, as I do, how reassuring it is to be in a room full of people and announce, along with everyone else, the equivalent of 'I dedicate myself to goodness.' Do it with your eyes open. Look around. Whether or not we have met before, we are all saying to each other, 'Relax. I am trustworthy.'" I often feel myself sigh—and even sometimes think I hear a collective sigh—as people look around and acknowledge what I experience as the gift of feeling safe.

I also invite people to listen to the sound as we chant or recite and to feel the pleasure in the body and mind that comes from saying familiar and heartwarming phrases. I feel my mind relax and become balanced with each repetition. That balance provides the antidote to the hypervigilant scrupulosity I feel—"Did I do that *exactly* right?"—when the level of alertness in my mind is high and the level of calm in it is low. When my mind is relaxed, I can trust my dedication to Morality, and my confidence in my good intentions is enough.

THE GOOGLE OF THE MIND

It's my experience that the relaxed, attentive mind, one filled with *sati* (Mindfulness), has the resources of Google, the Internet search engine that looks for everything everywhere. It is intuitive. It finds its way into places closed off to the linear mind. Just recently I was talking to a friend about Mindfulness entering into the language of religious traditions other than Buddhism, and I said, "There is a wonderful book written by a Jesuit priest who died not long ago, a student of S. N. Goenka, but I can't recall either the priest's name or the name of the book." An hour later, in the middle of doing something else, I thought, "His name was Anthony de Mello and the book was *Sadhana*." I had the distinct and pleasant feeling that some part of my mental faculty had gone off and looked up the answer from wherever it was stored in my archives.

It is also my experience that the same mental faculty that finds bits of buried information—Who was the Jesuit priest? Who was my second-grade teacher? Where did I leave my car keys? —uses its unassigned time to do routine "*karma* cleaning." It produces, on its own, unsolicited moral inventories.

The first time I saw that clearly was in the middle of a retreat at which I had been working hard, paying attention as carefully as I could, and realized that I felt, quite suddenly, wonderful. I was relaxed. I was alert. Practice, which had been effortful, was now easy. I recall feeling pleased with myself, and relieved, and incredibly happy. Quite soon, though, I noticed what seemed like a readout of mistakes I'd made—some recent, some not so recent—beginning to unfurl itself in my mind. "Where did *that* come from?" I thought. I was glad that my interview with my teacher was scheduled for that very day.

"I've done something wrong!" I told her.

"No, you didn't," she replied. "You're doing something right. Remember, Sylvia, this practice is called the Purification of the Heart. That's not for nothing. This *is* what happens."

Indeed. It is what happens. When I talk to my friends and colleagues, people who share Mindfulness, practice with me, they all have similar stories. "I couldn't believe it!" one of my friends said. "An entire retreat. As if I were on trial. The twenty most dreadful things I'd done in my life. And I feel like I'm a good person! I *am* a good person. It was humbling!"

It's meant to be. Humbling is not humiliating. It's remembering that we often don't know as much as we need to know in order to choose wisely. Spontaneous moral inventories of the attentive mind are reminders that, well intentioned as we may be, it's very easy to be distracted. *Hiri* and *otapa* are Pali words that mean understanding the possibility of causing suffering through heedlessness and understanding the very large ripple effect of every action. Both of those understandings inspire me to pay better attention.

On the second Wednesday of every month at Spirit Rock Meditation Center we have a special early morning class at which we use the Precepts as meditations. We sit together, quietly, for half an hour. Then I say the Precepts, one after another, in English, leaving a quiet space of several minutes between each one. As an instruction for people who might be coming for the first time, I say, before we start to sit, "When I say the Precepts, just listen to them. You don't need to *do* anything. They are a program for your mind to use while scanning its files, to let you know what you need to know."

After the meditation period, I invite people to talk about their experience. Often someone will say something like, "I was expecting to have the biggest connection with the Precept about incorrect speech. I've said some cruel things to my partner, and I've been feeling bad. But what really got to me was the Precept on taking what isn't freely given. What I got mad about with my partner was an old story, 'You're not meeting my needs,' and I realized that I've been demanding something not freely given. I could do better. I could ask."

Everyone's experience is unique, of course, but many people share the same realization: "I thought it would be this but it was that. Now I really understand what's going on. This is the part I haven't seen before. Now I think it can be different." What I've learned from my own experience, and from people sharing theirs with me, is that it doesn't matter if it is this or that Precept that catches the attention. They are all different ways to say "I'll do no harm." What matters is seeing things in a new way. When I began the Precepts meditation class many years ago, I imagined that reflecting on mistakes in the company of sympathetic friends who share our intention to perfect Morality would support our individual efforts to change our behavior. Now I think it does something greater. I think it supports our efforts to change our minds. I think Precepts practice, powered by *Mindfulness,* searches the mind to find information we have overlooked, information that could make us happy.

PRECEPTS IN THE MORNING: EVERYDAY MORALITY PRACTICE

A contemporary gratitude prayer making the rounds of meditation center bulletin boards reads: "I am thankful that thus far today I have not had any unkind thoughts or said any harsh words or done anything that I regret. However, now I need to get out of bed and so things may become more difficult." I am glad to use it as my "text" for inviting people to recite the Five Precepts out loud to themselves in the morning as they begin the work of their day. I say, "Maybe we should extend this prayer. We could add, 'And since things will surely become more difficult, and since I want to end the day thankful as well, I intend to:

> Do no harm to anyone,
> Take nothing that is not freely given,
> Speak truthfully and helpfully,
> Use my sexual energy wisely,
> And keep my mind clear.'"

The practice of recitation, even when I am alone, makes a difference to me. I am an out-loud witness to my good intentions, and I count on hearing my voice catch up with me during the day.

The Five Precepts are—along with other information important for me to see every day—taped to the frame of my computer screen, where I see them often. Many years ago, an artist friend and I laughed together about designing wallpaper with important Dharma written on it so we'd see it all the time, but we never did it. And the computer screen frame is fine as a reminder. I imagine the bathroom mirror would be another good place. I invite you to consider what would work for you.

CHAPTER THREE

Renunciation

/ /

Looking very deeply at life
as it is,
right now,
the person dedicated to awakening
dwells in stability and freedom.

The wise person calls someone
who knows how to dwell in Mindfulness
"One who knows the better way to live alone."
—THE BUDDHA

RENUNCIATION

The practice of:	Develops the habit of:	By:	And is supported by:	And manifests as:
Renunciation	Restraining	Realizing that insatiable wanting is suffering (the Second Noble Truth)	Discovering that everything passes, including uncomfortable desires (insight into impermanence)	Temperance

If I want to free myself from endless cycles of struggling with temptation—which the Buddha named in the Second Noble Truth as the root cause of suffering—I need to keep rediscovering that the pain of the struggle is greater than the pain of the desire. If I develop the habit of restraining myself, I'll enjoy the relief of feeling desires pass, and I'll remember that desires are not the problem. Feeling pushed around by them is. I'll continue to have desires, of course, because I am alive, but they'll be more modest in their demands.

✓✓✓✓

RENUNCIATION MEDITATION

Human beings have the amazing ability to not do something they feel like doing. It's a big accomplishment. The mind, just like life, is full of seductive Alice in Wonderland signs that say THINK ME! and DO THIS! The powerful gift of the practice of Renunciation is the capacity for restraint, the ability to read each sign as it comes into view and decide whether or not that's where you want to go.

Here's the meditation practice for developing restraint. First, restrain the impulse to turn the page and read on. In a moment, when you finish reading these instructions, you'll close your eyes, take some deep breaths in and out, and decide what particular focus you'd like to hold for the time that you sit. You could decide, for example, "I'll just feel the breath as it comes in and out at my nostrils" or "I'll just feel my chest expand and then relax with each breath" or "I'll just feel my belly rising and falling as each breath moves in and out of me." Decide that whatever you've chosen will be your single focus of attention. Then feel the impulse arise in the mind—as it very likely will—calling your attention to move to another part of the body or to become interested in thoughts or feelings. If you keep your attention fixed on whatever object of awareness you have selected, renouncing the impulse to change, it will be the mind equivalent of saying "Let's not go there." For three minutes, don't go there.

THE LANGUAGE OF SEDUCTION

Messages have begun to arrive in my e-mail with subject listings like "End-of-Season Bargains You Cannot Resist!" "Yes, I can!" I say to my computer screen and to the unseen sellers of something who have sent me the message, and I press Delete. I never peek. It's a matter of conscience. I'm not concerned that I'll accidentally be seduced into buying. And although I'd like to think that my refusal to even look is registering a vote on some worldwide level against moving the marketplace into people's homes, I think it only registers as an erasure in cyberspace. I do the same with messages I can identify as offering me information I already know, presented in a form that is designed to be inflammatory. That vote also, I am sure, does not count—except to me. I get to say, each time I avoid temptation, "Thank you very much, but I have everything I need." It's my practice. And it's a pleasure.

Twenty-five hundred years ago, in India, men and

women who were moved enough by the Buddha's message of freeing the mind from the insistent demands of greed and anger to dedicate their lives to that possibility became monks and nuns. It was the recognized, respected lifestyle for spiritual aspirants. The community supported it. And the lifestyle supported it. For monastics, a structured, simple, celibate life provided the possibility for discovering the pain of self-centered longing for personal choices and sensual gratification and the truth that those longings of the heart are temporary, that they pass, that the end of suffering is real. Renouncing the world—becoming a monk or a nun, living a life *designed* to steady the mind—was a powerful practice option. It still is.

I had fantasies—some years into my meditation practice, when I was able to recognize the habits continually churning up suffering in my mind, and when I'd had enough habit-free moments to know that a peaceful, compassionate, appreciative mind *is* a possibility—of "taking robes." They happened on retreat. I might be sitting, or walking, or drinking tea, and I'd have the thought "Everything is just fine." The thought was not connected to the fact that the meditation hall was very quiet, or the day was beautiful, or the tea was a lovely, new flavor. My *mind* was just fine. Poised. At ease.

I would give myself "alarm and dismay tests." I'd think about my daughter on holiday in Mexico. "What if Emmy forgot to take her asthma medicine?" And then I would think, "Probably she didn't forget. And they have pharmacies in Mexico. And I can't do anything about it." I would enjoy thinking about how much I loved her, how dear she is to me, and discover the pleasure of caring about her *without* being alarmed. Or to be sure that I still cared, that the feeling "Everything is just fine" was not a sign of indifference, I would think about the suffering in the world—wars, and poverty, and sickness, and the fact that half the world goes to sleep hungry. I would feel first pain and then the natural alarm that comes with pain. I would think, "It's definitely not okay. It needs to be fixed." And then, a bit later, "This is not a random world. Whatever happens has causes. These situations have causes. So they can be fixed. I'll help fix them." Resolve, held in steadiness—what the Buddha called "Clear Comprehension of Purpose"—frees the mind from the grip of fear that forms around the awareness "I *need* it to be another way." When I was able to restore my inner balance by remembering calmly, "This is what I *can* do, and I'll do it," I would think, "I need to be on retreat all the time. It keeps my mind from getting lost. I need to be a nun."

〜〜〜〜

Then the surprising daydream of a renunciation ceremony would begin. For some minutes I'd imagine—with pleasure—having my head shaved, taking vows, being given robes. The images always stopped on their own with the thought "I can't do that. That won't work in my life, at least not now." And then I'd think, "I'll have to be an invisible nun. I'll need to do my renouncing in my heart."

It is, after all, responding *unwisely* to greed and to anger that I want to renounce. Greed and anger, wanting and not-wanting, will happen for me forever, I think, as long as I am alive. They feel like a part of the natural response system of my mind and body. What I want to renounce is heedlessness. I want to remember, when I am being held in the uncomfortable thrall of impulse, compelled or confused, that freedom is a possibility.

The vow to renounce heedlessness is the inverse of the vow to pay attention. I have a verse from a song of an ancient Buddhist nun taped onto the frame of my computer screen. It reads:

I, a nun, trained and self-composed,
established mindfulness and entered peace like an arrow.
The elements of mind and body became still,
and I entered happiness.

I get to read it every time messages that incite or seduce appear in my mail. Online, at least, it helps me remember my choices. I'd like to think of it going with me when I am offline, in the rest of my life, as my nun's robe, as my habit.

ON MAKING VOWS

An experienced Mindfulness practitioner, a woman whose practice I know well, said to me in a retreat interview, "Here's the truth. I really do think I am much more attentive than I ever was before. And I can see that I have more space for reflection between thinking things and doing them. And I honestly think I am more softhearted. But I've discovered that I think absolutely *everything*. My mind is outrageous. These are *not* the thoughts I want to think. I cringe when I think them. I wish I could vow them away!"

We both laughed a little at her "confession," enjoying, I think, her trust in my affection for her, my holding her in good esteem, and her implied question, "Does that happen to you too?"

I said, "Everyone's mind is outrageous. And I think what happens with practice is that the increased ability to pay attention reveals more of what's going on. I don't think you are thinking more outrageously than before. You just know about it more." I told her that when I had asked that same question of U Sivali, a Burmese monk who had been my teacher at a retreat many years ago, he had said, "Pretend it's someone else's thought. It just floated into your mind. Leave it alone. It will float out."

And I suggested that she use the thoughts that dismayed her as Mindfulness objects. "Notice them," I said, "with as much kindness as you can. After all, you're already in pain from having thought them. Don't make the pain worse by cringing. You can't take a vow on thinking. You *can* try to renounce cringing. It would be the same as a vow to be mindful. Say to yourself, 'An ignoble thought has arisen in my mind. My mind has contracted. I am in pain. I am now taking a calm breath, paying attention to this breath in all its particularities, so that my mind can relax.' We could call this Mindfulness of Ignoble Thoughts. Maybe," I said, "we should add this specific category to the traditional Foundations of Mindfulness list. Then we could teach paying attention in the way that the Buddha taught—to our physical sensations, our emotions, our moods, our deepest experience of the truth—and, in a category all by itself, our ignoble thoughts." We laughed some more, agreeing about what a useful category this might be.

"Do it," she said. "It *will* help."

"I will," I replied, "next chance I get."

That evening in San Francisco I saw, closer than I ever had before, an accident in which a person was hit by a car in a crosswalk. It was terrible. I was one block away. I heard screeching brakes and then a thud. I stopped. The people around me stopped. Several people, I noticed, were immediately on their cell phones, and I guessed they were calling 911. Within a few minutes an ambulance, a fire truck, and paramedics had arrived, and I waited—as did the people around me— until the person who had been hit was taken away in an ambulance.

The next day I taught about using thoughts as meditation objects, especially the category of ignoble thoughts. I described the conversation I heard between members of a family, a mother and father and two sons, probably eight and twelve years old, standing next to me as we watched and waited after the accident the night before.

The youngest boy said, "I'm scared. Let's go home."

The older boy said, "Just be glad it isn't you."

The man said, "This is why your mom and I are always reminding you not to step out into the crosswalk without looking first, no matter what the light is."

The younger boy said, "I'm *really* scared. Let's go."

The woman said, "We'll go as soon as the paramedics come. I see two people with cell phones, and I think they've called for help, but we need to be sure."

I said to my class, "I had all the thoughts of all those four people—all by myself. I was frightened. I too wished I were at home. And I *was* glad it wasn't me. I thought, 'Five seconds later and it might have been me.' I resolved to pay more attention stepping off curbs. And I too was concerned that help be on the way, and I would not have left until the medical personnel arrived. I had the thoughts and feelings of a caring adult and the thoughts and feelings of an eight-year-old and probably everything else in between as well."

Then I said, "And I've been thinking about ignoble thoughts. Being glad it wasn't me was, I think, outside of the category of noble or ignoble. I think it was natural. The ignoble part was when I thought, 'Hmmm. This dialogue I'm hearing is exactly what I need to tell about the range of thoughts a mind can make.' I saw my mind, one second after the crisis had passed, leap back into self-serving mode."

"There wasn't anything else you *could* do, was there?" someone asked.

"I'm not sure," I said. "I guess I wish I had stayed tuned in to other people's needs at least a little bit longer. I'd feel I was a better person. But there it is. That's the truth. The trouble with Mindfulness is that you don't get anyplace to hide."

A week after the September 2001 attack on the World Trade Center in New York, I read from an article in *The New Yorker* to my Wednesday class. The author describes his responses to watching the TV news coverage—horror and sadness as well as disappointment at having his day disrupted, admiration for the planning that went into the attack, even an appreciation of the visual spectacle. He says, addressing his readers, that he imagines that many of them had those same thoughts, "unless you were a very good person indeed."

I said, "This is too solemn and sad a time for me to ask, 'Who here thought these same thoughts?' but I think this article is helpful."

A woman in the front row said, "I had all those thoughts. They just happened."

Other people nodded.

I said, "Here's what I think the connection is to our

being good, or even very good indeed. I think it's our goodness that recognizes those thoughts and says, 'Wow! Where did *that* come from?' I see that my mind is outrageous. Indiscriminate. It thinks *everything!* But my thoughts are not me. If I renounce any idea of ownership, they are free to leave."

REMINDING FORM

I work out in a great gym in Sonoma County, California. It is cheerful, well lit, and full of the latest innovations in exercise equipment. The latest arrival to the cardio fitness floor is a huge stationary bicycle with what looks like the movie screen part of an arcade video machine mounted on top of the handlebars. The exerciser mounts the bike, pushes a button to select a locale for the ride—South Sea Island Rim Tour, Tour de France (Pyrenees Section), Grand Canyon Ridge Ride—pushes another button to activate the movie, and starts pedaling. The road through the chosen location then unfolds on the screen, winding up and down and around corners with an image of a little biker weaving over the center line and then off onto the shoulder in response to the exerciser leaning to one side or the other. Relatively small untimely leanings translate on the screen into disappearing into trees alongside the road or falling out of sight off the edges of cliffs.

I enjoy watching how serious people become on the video bike, how important it suddenly seems to stay on the road, how hard they work to keep their attention up to speed. I do the same when it is my turn. Even in virtual reality, I enjoy feeling that I can restrain the impulse to distraction that might cause me to lose my balance.

I think of the various lifestyle choices I've made that are prescriptive dos and don'ts, choices that meet me regularly in the course of my everyday life, as roadside guardrails that keep me headed in the right direction. The rules—"This is what I do as morning practice," "This is what I do (or don't) eat," "I will not open my e-mail until I have done X," "This is what I think about when I get into my car before I turn the key"—serve as fences around my attention that keep me from blundering too far into the wilderness or falling into too much confusion. The rules themselves are secondary to their primary function. They all obligate me to stop. "Did I do that yet?" is not a checklist of completions. It is a wake-up call. "Am I about to do something that I have decided is unwise?" or "Am I paying attention?"

I cannot go far from my rules. Morning happens

every day. I eat every day. I drive a lot and e-mail a lot, but I have days set aside when I do neither, so I always need to remember what day it is and plan ahead. My friend James has, as a rule for his meditation practice, the obligation to at least sit on his *zafu* (meditation cushion) every day. His *zafu* is in his bedroom. If James finds himself about to get into bed at night without having "sat," he will. James says it doesn't matter how long he sits. He also says that the sight of his *zafu* is his visual equivalent of the "Mindfulness bell" rung at unanticipated times throughout the day in communities of students of the contemporary Buddhist teacher Thich Nhat Hahn. It reminds him to pay attention.

Ajahn Sumedho—an *ajahn* is a senior monk or nun in the Theravada Buddhist tradition—is the abbot of Amaravati Monastary near London. He grew up in southern California and after finishing university went to Asia to travel and study. In a discussion with other Mindfulness teachers—some monks, some nuns, and some (most of us) laypeople—about lifestyle practice choices, he said, "Thirty-five years ago, when I ordained as a monk, I thought I'd do it for two years. Then I discovered I liked the life. And besides, I like having a reminding form."

" 'Reminding form,' " I thought as I listened to Ajahn

Sumedho, "is just the right term to describe the structure of an intentional commitment." Any form sets limits. It mandates stopping: "Is this within my commitment or not?" And it requires promising. When "I promise to be true to . . ." is spoken as a Renunciation phrase, a public announcement of dedication to a practice or to a partner, it moves me to tears even when it is said by people who are strangers to me. I think about the trust required to make a promise or to believe one.

I struggle with my practice promises. For many years, when people asked at the end of retreats, "Do you sit every day?" I would say, "I try to. Really, though, it's not about sitting. It's about paying attention in every part of my life. Sitting is good for stabilizing my attention, but . . ." After however many years it took me to get ready to do it, I decided I wanted to have another answer. Now I say yes. I decided to have James's practice. The act of sitting down, even for a short time, with the intention to ask "Where am I? Have I lost my way? Am I still headed in the right direction?" is good for me. It reminds me of the promise of the Buddha: "I would not ask you to do this practice, to undertake this path of liberation from the habits of suffering mind, unless it were a feasible path. I promise you that it is." It reminds me that I believe it.

THIS DECISION IS JUST FOR NOW:
EVERYDAY RENUNCIATION PRACTICE

The point, for me, of my Renunciation practices is that they continue to teach my mind that the imperative it feels—"I *must* have this right now," "I *need* to do this my way"—is not true. The tension of desire in the mind is uncomfortable, but the lesson for me is always the same. The imperative passes—not because I have willed it away, talked myself out of it, or even promised it for later, but just because it passes, like everything else. It's thrilling (which is an odd word to use about a Renunciation practice) to be able to say, "I have desires, but I am not trapped by them."

I have some long-term lifestyle rules—a Sabbath day each week, particular foods that I do not eat—that have become so routine that they aren't a difficult practice for me. So I periodically take on new rules when they present themselves if I think they'll be helpful. Two years ago I gave a gift—larger than one I would normally do without asking Seymour, my husband—to a cause I support. I decided I would balance my unilateral decision by not buying fresh flowers on Friday afternoon for the next year, a long-standing habit pleasing primarily to me. "You really can buy flowers," Seymour said when I told him my plan. "It's fine about the gift. You don't need to balance."

It's been a good practice, though. I pass the flower shop as I do my Friday shopping. I stop to admire the display. I watch the flowers change with the seasons. Often I *feel* like buying some. I listen to my mind make up reasons: "It's been more than a year now." "These are *so* pretty!" "Tom and Mary are coming for dinner." "I really *should* be supporting the local flower growers." So far, I pass them by. The important lesson, one that is still working, happens when I am halfway down the street and realize that the tug at my heart that was present in front of the flowers is no longer there. Life is easier without imperatives.

Outside a vowed community with shared rules, everyone's life is different, and so I can't imagine what would be a valuable practice for you. But I invite you to think about choosing something you could give up, for some significant period of time, that you like enough so that you'd notice its absence but not so much that you or your family would be in discomfort. Then see what you learn. Remember, it's not about becoming stoic. It's about becoming intimate with the nature of desire itself. Desire pulls so *hard,* it's surprising to find that it's empty.

CHAPTER FOUR

Wisdom

////////////////////////////////////

> There are, O monks, these four splendors.
> What four?
> The splendor of the moon, the splendor of the sun,
> the splendor of fire and the splendor of wisdom.
> Of these four splendors, this is the best:
> the splendor of wisdom.
>
> There are, O monks, these four radiances . . .
> these four lights . . . these four lusters . . .
> these four sources of illumination.
> Of these four sources of illumination, this is the best:
> illumination by wisdom.
> —THE BUDDHA

The practice of:	Develops the habit of:	By:	And is supported by:	And manifests as:
Wisdom	Discerning	Understanding that although our minds are continually and inevitably challenged by desires, peace is possible (the First, Second, and Third Noble Truths)	Practicing Wise Effort, Wise Concentration, and Wise Mindfulness, the mind-training aspects of the Eightfold Path (the Fourth Noble Truth)	Clarity

If I pay attention, I see that all my experiences—pleasant, unpleasant, even neutral—are possibilities for grieving or resenting, discounting or worrying or doubting . . . possibilities for creating suffering. And I also see in those same experiences the possibility of maintaining a peaceful, contented mind if I cultivate positive mind habits (Wise Effort), steady attention (Wise Concentration), and balanced, clear awareness (Wise

Mindfulness). I trust that a growing ability to discern the possibilities for suffering and happiness as they arise in each moment of my life will keep me clear-minded and cause me to act with more Wisdom.

WISDOM MEDITATION

When I teach about Wisdom, the ability to know—deeply—the truth of how things are, I often hear decades-old echoes of my psychologist friends. Newly enthusiastic about the vocabulary of Gestalt psychology, they would ask, "How are you?" and when I replied, "I'm fine," they would follow up with "How are you, *really*?" At the time I thought they were being confrontational, maybe even impolite, and I'd feel annoyed. Now I understand that question as an invitation to look deeply under the surface of what is most apparent, and I teach a variation of it, "What's happening, *really*?" as a meditation instruction for the development of Wisdom.

The Buddha's sermon the Foundations of Mindfulness promises that paying attention in four specific ways—to physical sensations (beginning with the breath), to the affective tone of each moment of experience (pleasant, unpleasant, neutral), to the presence or absence of any specific state of mind (mind with or without anger; mind with or without calm; mind with or without any particular quality), and to what is deeply true about all experience—*guarantees* liberating Wisdom. The discovery that everything is always changing, that everything has multiple causes, most of them beyond our control, and that struggling to have things a certain way or to keep things a certain way is both futile and painful is the key, the Buddha taught, to developing the mind habit of noncontentious, gentle, wise response.

Here's how to do it. You can do this meditation with your eyes open, while reading these instructions, but please read *slowly* so you can feel what's happening as you go along. You're likely to be either sitting or lying down, so notice how it feels to be sitting, or lying down, and notice whether right now that feeling is pleasant, unpleasant, or neutral. Feel yourself breathing. Think the words that describe what's happening— "Breath is coming in," "Breath is going out," "This is a long breath," "This is a short breath," "This experience of breathing is pleasant," "This experience of breathing is neutral," or even "This experience of breathing is unpleasant." By thinking these words as if you were talking to yourself, you amplify your capacity for discernment, the hallmark of Wisdom. So try it. Close your eyes now, for a few minutes, so you can feel your body and your breath and practice telling yourself what's happening. Whenever you feel ready, you'll open your eyes and continue.

As you read on, staying aware of your body and your breath, think the words that describe the contents of your mind: "Mind with lots of thoughts in it," "Mind filled with energy," "Mind empty of energy (sleepy!)," "Mind filled with contentment," "Mind filled with restlessness," "Mind filled with delight," "Mind filled with irritability," "Pleasant," "Unpleasant," "Neutral." To develop Wisdom, it doesn't matter what mind state is present. It only matters that you know what is present.

Now that you've practiced telling yourself what's happening, spend some time telling yourself what's true about everything that's happening. (Here's the hint: It's all changing.) "A breath came in. Now a breath is going out." "My body was comfortable when I started this meditation. Now I want to stretch and move. Pleasant has become unpleasant." "I doubted I could meditate. That was unpleasant. Now I think I can. This is pleasant." "Everything changes!"

The next-to-last sentence that the Buddha is reported to have spoken as he was dying, before his final sentence of encouragement to his community, was

"Transient are all conditioned things." It means that everything that begins ends. Something else happens. This something else is dependent on what's happened before, but new. Knowing that everything is always changing supports the heart in times of difficulty, reminds it to celebrate every moment of joy, and keeps the mind awake, paying attention.

Try to meditate a bit longer now, with eyes open or closed. Ask yourself, "What's happening, *really*?"

NO COMPLAINTS

A delegation of twenty-six Western Buddhist teachers traveled to Dharamsala in 1995 for a week of meetings that included three days with the Dalai Lama at his palace residence. Three people who weren't Buddhist teachers—two video engineers who taped all the meetings and one journalist who was along as observer and possibly chronicler of the event—accompanied us. The three "outsiders" were introduced to the group on the first day, and it was agreed that they could stay in the room for all of the meetings but would not enter into any discussions. On the last day, after each of the teacher-participants had closed the meeting by mentioning what had been for them most meaningful, we asked the video engineers and the journalist for their impressions. The journalist said, "No one complained."

He was right. I hadn't thought of it before, but when he said that, I thought back over the many inconveniences of the whole week—not even including the tremendous effort required to get to Dharamsala, with long flights and overnight train rides, and bumpy, hair-raisingly dangerous taxi rides—and I realized, "Not once. No one complained." I particularly recalled the scene in which we were all walking back from the Dalai Lama's palace to our hotel for the midday meal in a driving rain with the water sluicing down the hill alongside us and across the road. I was sharing an umbrella with Ajahn Sundara, the most senior nun at Amaravati Monastery, both of us in sandals, sloshing along ankle deep in water, she trying to keep her robe up out of the water. No one complained. Not about that. Or the food. Or the schedule changes. Or the intense security searches each time we reentered the Dalai Lama's compound. Or about anything.

I felt very buoyed up by the journalist's comment. I felt as if we'd all gotten report cards in *Buddhadharma* (what the Buddha taught) and that we'd all gotten A's. One specific exam question would have been "What is the Second Noble Truth? What did the Buddha say was the cause of suffering?" We were all, by not complaining, demonstrating that we knew that suffering is caused by the mind demanding that things be different from how they are. And we were all, by accommodating, demonstrating the Third Noble Truth, "The end of suffering is possible." There are only two possible responses to every challenge—balanced acceptance or embittered resistance. Acceptance is freedom. Resistance is suffering. We all knew it.

I thought about the combined number of practice hours—indeed, years!—in the room, and I felt proud of us all. I wasn't sure it was only the hours on the *zafu* (meditation cushion) that accounted for our ability to stay balanced under pressure. Some people grow up in families that are more naturally courageous and resilient than others, and those folks clearly have a head start on Wisdom. But I trust that the conviction that becomes the very fiber of one's being comes from seeing over and over again that things are just what they are. Being able to hold whatever is happening as neither personal reward nor punishment short-circuits the mind's habitual tendency to struggle. Knowing that freedom depends on acceptance is what erases complaining. Complaining is, simply, unwise.

Pay Attention, for Goodness' Sake

UNCOMMON COMMON SENSE

One of my early meditation teachers began a lecture by saying, "Tonight I want to tell you about the special insights that you will be hoping to discover in your meditation practice—those insights that the Buddha taught were the key to liberation." When I heard this, I thought, "No! No! Don't tell me! That's not fair. That's like telling me the end of a mystery novel I've just begun. It'll take all the fun out it. And if I don't discover them myself, they probably won't count." The teacher went on, however, explaining what the Buddha taught as the Three Characteristics of Experience.

1. Everything is always changing (insight into impermanence).
2. Suffering is *extra* tension created in the mind when it struggles (insight into suffering).
3. Nothing has a substantive existence separate from everything else, or indeed any existence at all apart from contingency, apart from being the result of complex causes and a factor in subsequent experience (insight into interdependence).

I recall that after the lecture I wondered how discovering any of those characteristics by meditating would be different from thinking them as thoughts. After all, they weren't news. They sounded to me—at least to a part of me—like regular, garden-variety common sense, like something I thought I already knew. Some part of me, though, felt thrilled—as if I was hearing very good news for the first time. Something about the contentment and confidence and courage of my teachers communicated itself to me. As they taught about the liberation that the Buddha promised as the gift of profound understanding, I thought, "Whatever I already know, I could know better!" I got excited about meditating. It didn't matter that I thought I knew the insights in advance. I trusted that those very same insights—transforming insights that could liberate me—would arise mysteriously as revelations, in ways I could not yet imagine.

I'm glad I trusted. I do know better what I knew before, and I know it more of the time. I remember more consistently that although I try as hard as I can and hope as hard as I can, I am not in charge. Everything is always changing, and so nothing can be permanently satisfying. And I absolutely know that railing and resenting when I am displeased with life's unfolding compounds my pain. Life unfolds lawfully, guided by conditions far too complex for me to know and certainly far beyond my control. Those insights sounded right to me when I first heard them from my teachers, but hearing alone was not enough to change my mind's habit of resisting and struggling. I needed to meditate. I needed to pay attention. My habits of suffering—grieving, resenting, fretting—began to change when I could feel my mind, from one moment to the next, untie itself from a knot of painful struggle. Over and over again, each untying happened in a moment of clear seeing: "This is what's happening. It cannot be otherwise. Struggling is extra. Struggling is suffering." Each untying reroutes the mind in the direction of new wisdom in a way that makes enduring clarity seem a feasible albeit formidable task, like changing the course of the Mississippi one bucket of sand at a time.

This image of the Mississippi sustains me whenever my mind floods, when I am so shaken by events that I forget what I thought was firmly installed in me as Wisdom—when I suffer. I give myself time for the floodwaters to subside, for the confusion to sort itself out, for my mind to clear. I try to remember that I *used* to know. Or that my teachers, whom I love, know. Or that the Buddha—indeed, all the wise figures of all the great spiritual traditions—knew. Or, in fact, that *all* of us in our best moments also know. When we are relaxed and reasonably content, we are naturally wise. We accept that life is unpredictable, unreliable. We say jokingly or philosophically, "Nothing is sure except death and taxes," or "God willing and the creek don't rise," reminding each other that, notwithstanding the level of planning, we are continually dealing with being surprised. We get startled. We recover. We are disappointed. We adjust. Mostly—with Wisdom intact—we manage. When we are seriously challenged, though, when something happens that we so badly did not want that we can't bear to have it be true, we forget philosophy. Wisdom vanishes. We ask "Why me?" or, "Why now?" The pain we feel about what has happened intensifies with bitterness—which we often cannot help but feel—and we suffer. In a moment of Wisdom— "It *is* me. It *is* now. It *is* painful. And it will be painful for as long as it is, and then it will change"—the suffering stops. The heart's natural compassion becomes available to provide support, to comfort the pain.

These days I give more or less the same lectures— on retreat we call them Dharma talks (Wisdom talks in the tradition of the Buddha)—that I heard from my teachers. I teach the very same insights. Sometimes my teacher friends and I will urge each other on before the lecture, "Oh, good. You'll be talking about the Four

Noble Truths. Please do tell that story you always tell," and sometimes, playfully, "Please don't tell that same story again. Think of a new one. You've told it so often!" I sometimes begin a teaching talk by saying, "The name of this talk is . . ." and then mention a particular topic such as the Three Characteristics of Experience, the Four Noble Truths, the Five Hindrances—whatever basic template for Wisdom I'll use to shape what I say. Then I say, "But, you know, there is only one basic Dharma talk: How are we going to live this life, inevitably challenged, gracefully, with kindness and compassion?"

I *like* hearing—and giving—the same talks over and over. My friends and I do change the stories we tell to illustrate a point, but sometimes a good story lasts a long time. Often I find it pleasant to be hearing a familiar story because I know in advance the point it will be emphasizing, and I know that I will feel reassured. I resonate to what I know is true, and somehow—regardless of my particular circumstance—I feel consoled. And I enjoy teaching as much as I do because it gives me the chance to keep telling *myself* what's true. I often think that I deputize everyone I meet—unbeknownst to them—to tell me that same truth, lest I forget.

On a midwinter Sunday I stepped out of the apart-

ment building in which I was staying in upper
Manhattan and thought that everyone in New York
must have been watching the Giants-Vikings playoff
game on TV. The streets were empty and the first taxi
that came along stopped for me. The driver was listening to the game.

"You a football fan?" he asked as I settled into the
backseat.

"I am," I replied.

"Can I keep the radio on, then?"

"Sure."

We rode for a while. The Giants were ahead, 23–0,
and it was the beginning of the second quarter.

"It's not so much fun," I ventured, "when one team
is so much ahead. It's really all over."

"No, it isn't," the driver replied. "You never know.
Everything changes."

The big snowstorm of the week before had been
cleared away, and there was little traffic, so the drive
was smooth. I asked him how it had been to drive in the
storm.

"It was hard," he replied. "Were you here?"

"No. I live in California."

"Very smart," he said. Then he said, "Are you a palm
reader?"

I wasn't sure I'd heard right. "Excuse me?"

"Are you a palm reader?" he said again. "Or an astrologer? Or a psychic?"

"No." I laughed. "Why did you ask? Do I look a certain way?"

"No," he answered. "You look regular. But everyone in California is a little bit different in that way, you know what I mean?"

I thought for a while. "Matter of fact," I said, "maybe I do have an unusual job. I'm a meditation teacher."

"Aha! I *knew* it." He laughed, congratulating himself by slapping the steering wheel. Then he said, "What kind of meditation do you teach?"

"It's learning to pay attention," I said. "We practice paying attention all the time, not just at certain times. You don't need to be alone and you don't need to close your eyes. It's just calm, paying attention. Like I'm depending on you right now to be paying attention while you're driving."

"I'm always paying attention," he said. "What's the name of your meditation?"

"It's called Mindfulness."

"But does it have a tradition it's part of?"

"It does," I said. "It comes from Asia. The Buddha taught it."

"You a Buddhist?"

"I am," I said.

"So am I," he said. "You a monk?"

"No, I'm not," I said. "Who is your teacher?"

"He's a monk. He's got a long name. He has a center in my neighborhood. I go there every couple of months to hear him. He says some good things. Mostly I read books about Buddhism."

"I wrote some of them,'" I said.

"What's your name?"

"Sylvia Boorstein."

"Nope. Never heard of you. Here we are at Penn Station."

I was getting money out of my wallet to pay my fare and I heard the football score on the radio. The Giants' lead had increased. "You think this game is pretty much over now?" I asked.

He turned to see if I was being playful. I was. He smiled. "You *never* know," he said, exaggerating the "never." Then he laughed. "*Everything* changes."

I paid him, and as I got out I said, seriously, "I hope your practice thrives."

He answered seriously. "I do too." Then he laughed again. "Wait till I tell my wife *this* story! You never know."

LIFE *IS* CHALLENGING

In Pali, the word used in the First Noble Truth to describe the fundamental quality of life is *dukkha*. It's meant to convey the difficulty—since everything is always changing—of keeping our bodies and minds comfortable. It's often translated as "suffering" or "unsatisfactory." In English, though, the word *suffering* is close in tone to *miserable* or *horrible*—which isn't what the Buddha taught—and *unsatisfactory* sounds like a bad report card grade. *Challenging* comes closer to our experience. We are easily startled and easily frightened. And we are often heroic in our attempts not to frighten and demoralize each other.

In 1957 flying was still a novelty, and I recall the time my next-door neighbor Jerry Jacobson's elderly parents arrived in Topeka from New York for a visit that included their first-ever airplane flight. They recounted their experience with heroic pride.

"We wanted to sit next to each other," Jerry's mom said, "but they didn't have two seats together, so we sat in the same row across the aisle from each other."

"The stewardess said to us," Jerry's dad continued, " 'These are good seats. They are right over the wings, just behind the propellers. This is the most stable place to sit.' "

Jerry's mom finished the story. "We didn't know," she said, "that when the engines are working a rosy glow comes out the back of them. So, not long after the plane took off, I said to Dad, 'Are you okay?'

"He said, 'I'm okay. Are you okay?'

"I said, 'I'm okay.' We both noticed the rosy engine exhaust.

"We flew a bit farther. I saw Dad glancing out his window. I looked out mine.

" 'Still okay?' I checked.

" 'I'm okay,' Dad said.

"Finally he caught on and said, 'Listen, I won't tell you that my engine is on fire if you don't tell me your engine is on fire.' "

People usually laugh when I tell that story, partly, I think, because it's a sweet story about an old couple keeping each other's spirits up. But I think there is another, more universal reason for the laughing: We recognize ourselves in the story. Mostly we go about our days behaving as if nothing is awry, caring for our bodies and our relationships and our work projects as if everything is fine, as if our engines are not on fire. Maybe we're afraid to tell ourselves, or embarrassed to tell anyone else, that our life is challenging. It seems to keep slipping our minds that the difficulties we keep running into are not personal flaws, that there really *isn't* some way to get everything just right and keep it that way, that challenges—one after another—are what life is.

I was talking to my friend and Spirit Rock teacher-colleague Julie Wester at a time when both of us were grieving about events that were happening in our families. We heard each other out and agreed that in both our situations there was nothing apart from telling the truth and having it heard by a friend that could be done. We were both frightened. We were both suffering. The respectful hearing, I think, legitimized the suffering. We didn't need to "rise above it" and we didn't need to feel ashamed.

Julie said, "You do remember, Sylvia, don't you, that the Buddha said, 'Everything that is dear to us causes pain'? He was right!" We both laughed. The Buddha *was* right. It is the very dearness of things that makes us vulnerable to the inevitable pain of change, of disappointment, of loss. And it *is* wryly comical for Mindfulness teachers who regularly explain the Buddha's wisdom about the fundamental challenges that are part of being a human being with a body and with relationships—bodies that change and relationships that change—to be in the position of reminding each other, as if we didn't know. We *do* know.

Everyone knows. Everyone who is paying even the least bit of attention and who has ever been disappointed knows that caring makes us vulnerable. And we keep going on ahead, cultivating connections. It's a human characteristic—one we are glad to have—to make investments of the heart, to care. We do it naturally. By the time we figure out, "Wow! Caring has made me vulnerable to pain," it's too late for anything but compassion, for anything other than staying present to remind friends, or be reminded by them, that this is life: beyond our control but lawful, often difficult but also manageable and bearable.

When Julie and I laughed together—having reminded each other of the truth of suffering—we both noticed that the energy in our voices had come back. Not hiding from suffering is a relief. Then the pain of the situation is just what it is, but not more. The mind, freed from the grip of struggle, is able to remember what it already knows, that everything changes, and it gets a chance to rest. Perhaps Julie and I reminded each other— if we didn't, we could have—that the Buddha also said that the Dharma, like a bird, needs two wings to fly, and that the wing that balances Wisdom is compassion.

AN ATTACHMENT NAMED DESIRE

I heard on the CBS Radio 7:00 A.M. news—the broadcast my husband, Seymour, says has the most important information of the day—that a tourist at Kilauea National Park in Hawaii had fallen over the rim of the volcano chasing after his baseball cap, which had been blown off by the high winds. Had his fall not been broken by a tree growing out of the side of the volcano fifty feet below the top, and had the helicopter pilot and the paramedics not succeeded in their rescue mission, the tourist would have died chasing his hat. The headline for the story was "What Is a Baseball Cap Worth?" As I listened to the details, I thought, "Maybe it was Joe DiMaggio's hat. Or Mickey Mantle's hat." I realized immediately how ridiculous a thought that was. No one's hat is worth your life, and surely the poor tourist wasn't thinking he needed his hat more than his life. He just wasn't looking where he was going. But still, it makes a good parable for showing the possible perils of becoming confused by what we think we need.

Tanha, the word the Buddha used in the Second Noble Truth to define the cause of suffering, is usually translated as "craving." I feel it in myself as unappeasable wanting—wanting so much to have something

I don't have, or wanting so much to have something I do have but I don't want to go away—that my mind cannot rest. The having, or not having, becomes such a large preoccupation that it fills the mind with the painful energy of greed or aversion. Clear seeing is impossible. Attempts to talk myself out of my need are useless. They tie the mind into even tighter knots of recrimination and despair. In order for the mind to relax, it needs to be reasonable. Caught in the grip of unappeasable need, it's hysterical.

Recognizing that neediness is suffering, feeling the pain of longing in both the mind and the body, is what begins to untie the knots. We are, after all, wired to be compassionate. We pick up and soothe children who trip playing hide-and-seek, who stumble and hurt themselves thinking they need to find someone or hide from someone. We don't scold them. We know they've stumbled because the game is real for them and—at that moment—very important. It's not much different for us as adults. In the middle of a game of lust-and-aversion, the real world—the only world in which loving connection is possible—disappears. Whenever we stop the game— by realizing what a rough game it is and how much we are hurting ourselves by staying in it—we rejoin the real world.

The Buddha is quoted as saying, "I've come to teach one thing and one thing only: suffering and the end of suffering." The Second Noble Truth, "Suffering is unappeasable need," has both the cause of suffering and, by implication, the end of suffering folded into one sentence. It's an enormously valuable sentence. It's the core of the Buddha's teaching, the essence of his Wisdom. And it's the sentence before the Third Noble Truth, the most liberating good news: "Peace is possible!" Imagine how it would be in our present world if someone were to announce positive proof that peace—and its derivative, happiness—is possible for everyone in this very life no matter how their bodies are or what their circumstances may be. It would certainly be the most important information of the day and be part of the CBS Radio 7:00 A.M. news. Maybe they broadcast the story about the tourist at Kilauea National Park so we would remember not to lose our lives chasing our hats.

A SATISFIED MIND

I like gospel music. I keep a cassette tape of Loretta Lynn singing gospel in my car and I play it—loud—and sing along with it. I find it reassuring, and kind, and full of good Dharma. My favorite song on this particular tape is "A Satisfied Mind." The lyrics describe the priceless quality ("more valuable than silver or gold") and the enduring quality (unlike "fortunes [that] may crumble") of a satisfied mind. The last line of the song is amazingly confident: "There's one thing for certain . . . I'll leave this old world with a satisfied mind!"

I'd like to leave this world with a satisfied mind, and I'd like to have one, as much as I am able to, while I'm still here. The Third Noble Truth, the Buddha's promise that a peaceful, contented, nonstruggling, satisfied mind is a possibility in this very life, is unequivocal and simple. The practice discipline for achieving that mind, the Fourth Noble Truth, the Eightfold Path, is clear, comprehensible, feasible and—because it requires paying attention all the time to thoughts, to actions, to inclinations, to intentions, to *everything*—demanding. A full-time commitment. I ask myself, though, "What's the alternative?" I heard that Trungpa Rimpoche, founder of the Naropa Institute, a major Buddhist center in Boulder, Colorado, often ended the first day of a retreat, when new students might be tired and bewildered, by saying, "I imagine that many of you would like to go home now." He would pause and then say, "Too late." I've assumed that Trungpa

Rimpoche meant that on retreat or off retreat, it's too late, once we know it's *possible* to live contentedly, to not try to learn how to do it.

Perhaps it was wise pedagogy on the part of the Buddha to teach the training discipline as eight different practices—Wise Understanding, Wise Intention, Wise Speech, Wise Action, Wise Livelihood, Wise Effort, Wise Concentration, Wise Mindfulness—with separate, specific instructions. Perhaps deciding "I'll start with study and prayer as a way of generating enthusiasm for meditation," or "I'll start with meditation, develop concentration, and then see what happens" is less daunting than saying "I'll consider my whole life as my practice." The truth, though, is that each of the eight different practices is its own particular doorway into the whole of life. Each one is a particular permutation of mindful awareness. Each single practice is designed to help the mind unlearn its tendency to struggle and habituate it to peaceful response. They are all iterations of the fundamental instruction, "Pay attention." When we aren't paying attention we are easily bewildered.

A sixth-grade student, a friend of my grandson Collin, asked me, "How can I *know* when I'm not paying attention? I *think* I'm paying attention in school, but then later I find I missed a lot." I'm not sure how I answered him. I certainly understood his question, but he came to mind on an airplane trip some time later, in a moment in which I thought, *"That's* the answer," so I'm guessing that whatever I said, I wasn't as sure of it then as I was on the plane.

I was flying home to California from Boston after several weeks of teaching Mindfulness retreats. I noticed, once the plane was airborne, that although I had the *New York Times* in my lap and the sweater I was knitting for my granddaughter Grace in my bag under the seat in front of me, no impulse arose in me to read or to knit, or indeed to do anything. "I'm maxed out," I thought. "I'm like a computer with limited memory and I've used it all up." I realized, somewhat ruefully and probably because the thought was so dramatically bizarre, that my mind, in its habitual way, had once again created a crisis out of nothing.

I looked around at my traveling companions. The man next to me clicked away busily at his laptop, his eyes wide open, his gaze fastened on the screen. Next to him, slumped against the window, wrapped in a blanket pulled over the head, someone was asleep. I felt an affectionate intimacy with these two strangers who were sharing this cramped space thirty-five thousand feet above the ground with me. My mind drew frames around them, imagined them as two illustrations for a Dharma talk on the Five Hindrances (afflictive emotions that cloud the mind) and wrote James Thurber captions under each one: (1) Restless Man with Mind Full of Anxious Energy and (2) Torpor Man (or Woman) with Mind Empty of Energy.

The flight attendants distributed lunch. The blanket-body unwrapped itself and the woman inside it unwrapped her meal and began to eat. I began to eat. No one spoke. I looked across the aisle to my left. A man I judged to be in his late twenties was eating his lunch and watching the video on the small screen in front of him. I noticed that his earphones looked unusual, and then I saw that although he was *watching* the video, he was *listening* to a CD player. A fork was in his right hand, and an open paperback novel was in his left. He was holding the book up at the level of the screen so he could look back and forth easily. My mind cartoonist drew a box around him and noted Lustful Man with Mind on the Verge of Exploding.

I laughed out loud, startling myself by my outburst, and then, aware of the man next to me, I wondered, "What can he be thinking about me, laughing all of a sudden seemingly in response to nothing?" Then I had an age-conscious thought: "Probably he thinks that I do odd things because I'm old." I felt embarrassed. I sat up taller, took a deep breath, looked back at the young man across the aisle, and understood clearly that he was frightened.

I realized then that I was frightened too. I'd been worried just a moment before about whether the man next to me had judged me as eccentric. And before that I'd been mildly worried—at least enough to notice it—that my lack of interest in the newspaper and knitting was a sign of mental overload, or worse, declining vigor destined to drop even more with time. Then I told myself the bigger truth: "I really don't like flying. I'm *okay* about it, it's not a *problem,* but I don't like it."

I looked back at the young man I'd just laughed at and felt touched by how hard he was working to keep himself comfortable. "May you be happy," I wished for him. "May you be peaceful." I wished the same for the man next to me and the woman next to him. Recovering my own kindness comforted me. I wished the same for myself. Perhaps that was the moment in which I knew the answer to Collin's friend's question: "I know I'm not paying attention if I am not feeling kind."

The rest of the trip was easier. I behaved wisely. I paid attention to keep my mind clear. I could remind myself, "I am tired, but not irrevocably. I don't *need* to do anything. Praying for all of us is enough." I felt satisfied.

ASKING BETTER QUESTIONS

The Buddha lived for more than eighty years. The five ascetics that he taught on the road to Benares became the first people to acknowledge him as their teacher. They "asked for refuge," which means they became monks in the community that he would lead. As the Buddha traveled and taught, many other men joined the order of monks. When women asked for refuge, an order of nuns was founded. As word of the wisdom of the Buddha's teaching, the peacefulness of his demeanor, and the depth of his compassion became widespread, people began to imagine him a deity. In one story, an awestruck person asked: "Are you a god?"

"No," the Buddha replied.

"Are you some other kind of celestial being?"

"No," the Buddha replied again.

"Are you, then, a plain man?"

"No," the Buddha replied for the third time.

"What *are* you, then?" the person asked.

The Buddha said, "I am awake."

I often tell that story when I teach, to give instructions for Mindfulness as well as to remind people of the goal of practice. I say, "The Buddha said, 'You should be alert enough to know when you wake up whether you have woken up inhaling or exhaling. And when you fall asleep, you should be able to tell if you've fallen asleep inhaling or exhaling.'" People are usually surprised and often skeptical. Those are, they remind me, the *least* likely times to be clear about what's happening. That allows me to say that I think the instruction is not about the morning and evening times that we generally associate with literally waking up and falling asleep. My experience has been that it is possible for me to "fall asleep," or zone out, throughout the day while doing routine tasks—including the routine but complicated and potentially dangerous task of driving my car. I can do it in conversation with another person. I haven't ever hurt anyone by my driving, but I've hurt feelings very badly when I haven't been paying attention. I think the Buddha's instruction is "Pay attention all the time!"

To emphasize the goal of practice, I go back to the story of the awestruck questioner and say, "I wish he would have asked one more question. He could have asked, 'What do you see that I *don't* see now that you are awake?' And I can imagine the Buddha responding, 'I see how much suffering there is in the world, and I see that its remedy is compassion.'"

Sometimes I tell the story of being picked up very early one morning at a retreat center in Santa Barbara by a van taking people to the Los Angeles airport. The back of the van was full of quiet, sleepy-looking passengers, so I sat up in front next to the driver. I recognized him. He had driven me from Los Angeles to Santa Barbara the week before, when the van had been empty, and we had talked all the way. I knew that his name was Mohammed, that he had come to Los Angeles from Bombay some years previously, that his wife and mother and two sisters and three brothers were still in India awaiting visas, that the restaurant he had opened with a cousin in Ventura had failed, and that he was hoping that driving a van would be only an interim job. He smiled at me to let me know that he remembered me, and—because it was still dark and the people in the back seemed to be sleeping, and also because I had used up all the conventional questions—I sat quietly. One hour into the two-hour trip, he leaned over and whispered to me, "Do you think it would be all right if I pulled off the highway at the next place we see a rest stop to get myself a cup of coffee? I'm really sleepy."

I said, "I'm *sure* it would be all right. In fact, maybe you'd like me to drive until we get there."

He said, "No, I'm all right. In five or ten minutes there'll be a place."

I decided I would engage him in conversation to be sure he stayed alert, so I turned in my seat to face him, searched my mind for a new topic, and said, "Mohammed, I am assuming you are a Muslim. Is that right?"

He said, "Yes, I am."

"Do you pray?" I asked.

"Yes, of course."

"Every day?"

"Yes, of course."

"Five times a day?"

"Yes, of course."

And I said, "What do you say when you pray?"

He shrugged. "I don't know it in English."

"Don't tell me in English," I replied. "Tell how you say it."

He said, "Okay, this is what I say . . . ," and he spoke for a while in Arabic.

"Do you need a certain number of people to pray?" I asked when he was done.

He said, "No, any number. You can pray by yourself, or you can pray with a lot of people."

"How long does it take to pray?"

"Well, it could take long or it could take short. If you have a short time, you can do it in a short time. Probably longer is better." He paused, as if he was thinking about it. Then he said, "You know, it really doesn't matter how long you pray. Some people stand and pray all day but it doesn't really count because it's not connected to their heart."

I said, "Really? How do you connect it to your heart?"

"Well, you can't just decide. It gets connected to your heart when you know what the situation here is." He waved his arm broadly, indicating the world going by outside the van. "It's like we've all been thrown in the middle of the ocean. Nobody knows how to swim. We're all drowning. It breaks your heart. You see that, then you connect."

At that point I said, "Mohammed, I see a Wendy's over there. Do you want to get off and pick up some coffee?"

He said, "No, I'm awake."

Wisdom

"THEY LOVE IT WHEN I AM A BUDDHA": EVERYDAY WISDOM PRACTICE

I often teach daylong classes in retreat form. I begin the day by setting an intention for our work together: We acknowledge each other as a practice community; we often recite the Precepts; and we agree to keep "retreat silence," taking part in group discussions and asking questions but not "visiting." At midday, since people bring lunch with them and eat alone, keeping the silence (outdoors if the weather is good), I like to say, "Here is a brief instruction, not exactly the formal instruction for mindful eating, but appropriate for the work we are doing today: Eat your lunch like a Buddha. Then, if you can, take a walk. Walk like a Buddha. Come back when you hear the bell, and we'll practice together for the afternoon."

Everyone seems to understand that instruction. No one has yet asked, "What do you mean? How should I do that? How *can* I do that? I'm not a Buddha." I think the question gets in under the radar of the rational mind and speaks to the part of us that *knows*. I don't think it would work for me to say, "Eat wisely" or "Walk like a sage." All of us would feel self-conscious.

So here's the everyday practice: Do your day, whatever you're doing, like a Buddha. The people you meet will probably appreciate you. You'll feel good. And you don't need to tell anyone what you're doing. Twenty years ago, even ten years ago, when Buddhism was not widely known in the United States, students at Mindfulness retreats often said, "My family is uneasy about what I'm doing here. They worry when they think I am a Buddhist, but they love it when I am a Buddha."

CHAPTER FIVE

Energy

///////////////////////////

It is this way that we must train ourselves:
by liberation of the self through love.
We will develop love,
we will practice it,
we will make it both a way and a basis,
take a stand upon it,
store it up,
and thoroughly set it going.
—THE BUDDHA

The practice of:	Develops the habit of:	By:	And is supported by:	And manifests as:
Energy	Striving	Realizing that there is no time other than now (insight into interdependence)	Focusing on the formidable task of ending suffering, and remembering the possibility of peace (the First and Third Noble Truths)	Indefatigability

I feel an invigorating consolidation of my Energy—a striving to *be here now*—each time I realize that *now* is the only time anything happens and that *every* now, disappearing just as rapidly as it arrives, has been shaped and created by a habit and—in its fleeting existence—is shaping and creating habits. I know that my experience of a peaceful, happy mind depends on developing the habits that support it. Since habits are, by definition, deeply ingrained patterns, and all moments are immediately lost, I need to enlist every moment to teach me about suffering and the end of suffering. Knowing that I haven't a moment to lose keeps my Energy level high.

ENERGY MEDITATION

In the Hollywood comedy about beauty pageants, *Miss Congeniality,* all but one of the contestants give the same answer to the question "What do you wish for most?" They say, "World peace." The maverick contestant wishes for something personal for her own happiness, and then, faced with a silent, shocked audience, adds, "*And* world peace." We laugh at that scene, as we do through the whole movie, at being shown the emptiness under the glitter and the enormous energy being expended to win recognition for beauty that is artfully, but artificially, enhanced and ultimately bound to disappear. We take pleasure in seeing that the pageant is theater— all padding and primping and practiced responses that no one actually believes. Maybe we also laugh because the joke makes us a bit anxious, the way good humor ought to, and we become nervous. What do *we* wish for most? What rouses our Energy? What if "world peace" *is* the winning answer, but we know in our heart of hearts that personal peace is what we wish for most?

Here is reassuring news, and a meditation to go with

it. It is our own pain, and our own desire to be free of it, that alerts us to the suffering of the world. It is our personal discovery that pain can be acknowledged, even held lovingly, that enables us to look at the pain around us unflinchingly and feel compassion being born in us. We need to start with ourselves.

Try to read these instructions slowly all the way through before you begin so that you'll be able to meditate with your eyes closed. Plan to spend the first two or three minutes of your meditation time resting your attention simply in the coming and going of your breath, letting your breathing rhythm be natural and easy and letting your body relax. Then ask yourself the questions "What do I wish for most? What do I most wish were other than how it is? What is the source of my greatest pain?" Feel what happens in your body and in your mind as you respond to that question. It's likely that your response will be habitual, familiar. Try not to think about it. Try to *feel* it. Remember to check in with your breathing, using the regularity of the breath to steady you through your direct insight into suffering. Sit as comfortably as you can. Breathe. Rest. Sit long enough for your body and mind to relax again.

By doing this, you just learned a lot. You discovered that being directly in the middle of the truth—even if the truth is unpleasant—is manageable. You just sat through the awareness of what is most painful to you. And even if you struggled a little bit and your mind and body became tense, to whatever degree you were able to relax again you learned that suffering comes from struggling, and that stopping the struggle is possible. And because you discovered—by doing it, not by thinking about it—that nonstruggling acceptance ends suffering, you learned that *now* is the only time it's ever possible to unlearn habits of suffering. For myself, the awareness that I have a limited number of nows creates a sense of urgent striving. It restores my Energy.

TIME OFF

At the first of what have now become regularly scheduled meetings of Western Dharma teachers with the Dalai Lama to discuss questions of interpreting Buddhism in our culture, one of the Western teachers said, "Here is a problem I have. So many people have become interested in Buddhism that I am teaching all the time. I have no time off." The Dalai Lama speaks English well but was not familiar with the term "time off." He leaned over toward his interpreter and they had a vigorous discussion, back and forth, as the interpreter apparently needed several chances to reformulate the meaning of the idiom so that it was understood. Suddenly the Dalai Lama laughed—a robust, cheerful, impish laugh—and turned back to the person who had asked the question.

"Do bodhisattvas [saints] get time off?" he asked.

Everyone laughed. The Dalai Lama is known for his intense teaching and traveling schedule, for his tireless work on behalf of freedom for all people. And he is playful. I thought, "*He* doesn't rest, but his mind does. He has taken a holiday from suffering. That's what gives him his Energy."

I think about the way in which fully attending to the pain in the world and resolving to end it energizes the mind. Perhaps it is paying attention that creates passion, making us truly alive in our lives for however long we live. Maybe it even extends our lives.

Kalu Rimpoche, a respected teacher in the Kagyu lineage of Tibetan Buddhism, led several hundred people in the Bodhisattva Initiation vow at the Franklin Street Unitarian Church in San Francisco in 1984: "Although suffering is endless, I vow to end it; although beings are numberless, I vow to liberate them."

Kalu was an old man, well into his nineties. His manner was simultaneously regal and beguiling. He spoke in

Tibetan, through an interpreter, but he seemed so connected to all of us that I hardly noticed.

"You don't need to be nervous about taking this vow," he said, "because a vow with a guru only lasts for the guru's lifetime, and I am old. I'll die soon, so the vow will be over. And don't worry," he continued, "if you have another religion. Caring about suffering doesn't only happen to Buddhists. Everyone wants to end suffering. And if this vow sounds like an impossible contradiction, don't worry about that either. It's okay."

What mattered most to me was his reassurance about the consequences of breaking the vow. "Don't worry," he said, "about making a mistake. You definitely will. Nothing bad will happen to you. The important thing is to make the intention, to want to serve all beings, to dedicate yourself to liberation."

I remember being moved by the eagerness and earnestness of everyone in the church. The pews were full. People lined the aisles and stood along both side walls. I recall thinking that Buddhism was becoming more mainstream in America, less counterculture. Ten years before, everyone I met on retreat seemed a generation younger and hipper than I was. Now the people around me in the church looked like me.

Kalu Rimpoche chanted the bodhisattva vow. We sat

and stood and then sat again, with intervals so that people who wanted to do prostration bows (kneeling and then stretching the body out full length on the floor to signify respectful commitment) could move past the others in their pews to get into the aisles to bow and then get back to their places before the next chant began. The narrow space between the pews and the number of people needing to get in and out made the logistics complicated. I could imagine another circumstance, one in which the goal of practice was not so clearly enunciated, where the scrambling of people in and out and around each other might have seemed funny. This was serious, though. Somehow, through the language barrier and across the culture gap, everyone seemed to connect with the intensity of the awareness of suffering and the desire to end it, with the Energy of shared, devout intention.

"IT'S YOUR LIFE, DON'T MISS IT!"

Until quite recently, no one ever challenged me when I said that the Buddha said, "We ought to practice as if our hair is on fire." I thought it was a good metaphor for the Energy level needed to meet the lifelong challenge of keeping the mind clear, remembering what's important, refining the capacity of the heart for goodness. Then a young woman came to see me during lunchtime at a daylong Mindfulness workshop. She said, "That's an awful image. It's so frantic." She reminded me that Thich Nhat Hanh says, "Life is so short, we should all move more slowly."

When I taught again in the afternoon, I went back to the hair-on-fire metaphor and suggested that I thought it had to do with urgency and not alarm. I told the group how inspired I had been when one of my teachers—describing how easily we are caught up in rehearsing for the future or ruminating over the past, all the while not awake to present experience, not choosing wisely—had said, "It's your life. Don't miss it!" I wanted to tell a story about what being awake to present experience means, and immediately thought of a famous one from the Zen tradition.

A tiger gave chase to a monk who had been walking peacefully near a cliff, and the monk, running as fast as he could, had no choice but to leap off the edge of the cliff to avoid being eaten. He was able, as he leapt, to grab hold of a vine trailing over the cliff and dangle in midair with the tiger snarling at him overhead and under him a very long fall into a rushing river full of boulders. Then he noticed a mouse gnawing at the vine. He also noticed, growing out of a cleft in a rock in front of him, a strawberry plant with one ripe berry. He ate it. He said, "This is a very good strawberry."

The monk's situation is a dramatic example of everyone's situation. We are all dangling in midprocess between what already happened (which is just a memory) and what might happen (which is just an idea). Now is the only time anything happens. When we are awake in our lives, we know what's happening. When we're asleep, we don't see what's right in front of us.

A year after my husband and I were married, we moved to Kansas. To our extended families in New York and New Jersey, Kansas was impossibly far away. We developed the habit—maintained through all of our moves and all these years—of including a recent photo of us in the New Year greeting that we send each year, so that our relatives would feel that we were staying in touch. As our family grew, the photo went from two people, to three people, to four, then five, then six. Then the number of people in the photo stayed the same for many years, but the children in it got bigger and everyone in it got older. By and by, as my sons and daughters chose life partners, more people joined the photo. They had children, and then even more people were in the photo. With increasing years and increasing people, the project of taking the August photo, which had begun as simply as "Let's step out into the backyard for a minute," became more elaborate. It required a lot of advance planning to coordinate schedules.

The photo taking, in a recent year, happened just under the wire for sending the greeting cards on time. I brought the film to the photo shop early the next morning, went for an hourlong bike ride while the pictures were being developed, and then went back to the photo shop to choose the best of them to make duplicates for the cards.

The photos were great. Several of them had all of us smiling. I picked the one I thought was best.

"How many prints do you need?" the saleswoman asked.

It was then that I realized that I didn't need *any*. Everyone we had needed to send photo greetings to— parents, aunts, uncles—had all died. I felt genuinely surprised and a bit embarrassed. I had explained to her earlier that I needed the prints developed promptly so I could send my cards on time.

I thought of whom else I could send a card to. I have two cousins. Seymour has a few. My friends have varying views about the political correctness of supporting the culture's use of religious holidays for mercantile gain, and they mostly don't send cards. My children's in-laws? That seemed like a good idea. They would, I thought, enjoy seeing the whole family.

Just then I realized that I was trying very hard to wring the last bit of possible pleasure out of a situation that didn't exist anymore. The trying was tedious. I also realized that the increasing effort, each year, to get everyone together in a good mood to take a photo had become tedious.

"I don't need duplicates after all," I said, indicating the display of our family pictures in front of me on the counter. "So many of these are fine. I'll have enough for everyone."

I walked through the parking lot on my way to my car feeling dismayed about my whirlwind, enthusiastic attempt to orchestrate a project without a cause, and thinking, "How can I not have noticed before now that the list of relatives is down to nothing? All of those people didn't die in the last year." An hour before, I'd been riding my bike, feeling energetic and vital, and now, quite suddenly, I felt old. I started to tell myself a sad story about how tired I was from rushing around, and then I realized, "No, I'm not. That's not true. I'm *not* tired. I'm startled to find that so much of my life has happened, that all my older relatives have died, that I am—if things go as they should—next in line in this family for dying. But not yet. Now I'm alive." I laughed as I saw that I had almost been trapped by my chagrin and dismay—they both siphon Energy out of the mind—into missing my opportunity. I turned around, went back to the photo shop, and found the same saleswoman.

"I'm back," I said. "I decided I want an eight-by-ten of the one I liked best."

As she was writing up the order for the enlargement, she looked up at me and said, "Eight-by-ten?"

I said, "No. I changed my mind. Eleven-by-fourteen."

She smiled. "Are you sure?"

I said, "Yes. I'm sure. This is a very good photo."

THE BEST POSSIBLE INCARNATION

The world into which the Buddha was born had, as a cosmology, a hierarchy of realms of incarnation and a universally accepted belief in cycles of rebirth. In that system, the realm of human beings is in the middle—lower than angels and deities, higher than animals and "all those in woeful realms." The Buddha taught that the likelihood of a human birth is as rare as the likelihood of a giant sea turtle—one that surfaces only once in an eon—raising its head through the one single ring (which I imagine as a lifebuoy) that is floating on all the oceans of the earth. Very rare. He also taught that a human life—able to sense sorrow as well as happiness—is the most precious of all lives. Understanding both the truth of suffering and the possibility of the end of suffering, the Buddha said, provides the motivation for staying connected and for perfecting goodness in spite of life's difficulties. Understanding how quickly a human lifetime passes *and* how rare it is inspires the Energy for using every moment of it well.

I started a conversation not long ago with a woman in the airport in Newburgh, New York, by saying, "Are you going somewhere to visit or are you going home?" I was waiting for my flight to Chicago. She had come from Chicago and was waiting for her connecting flight back to West Virginia. I had noticed that when the young man with her had settled her into the seat next to mine saying, "Stay here, Grandma. I'll go get you a Pepsi," she had just sat. Not reading. Not looking around. Not rummaging in her purse. Not doing any of the things people do in airport boarding lounges.

"I'm going home," she responded. "And this is only the second time I've flown anywhere. Flying here the day before yesterday was the first time." She half turned her face to me and spoke quietly but seemed glad to talk—more shy than nervous.

"Why did you come?" I asked.

"My granddaughter was getting married, so I really needed to come." We talked for a while about the wedding. I asked about the church, the service, the minister, the bride's dress, and the wedding cake, and each time she smiled, her face still turned only partly toward me, and told me something particular enough to let me know that she was enjoying our conversation.

Then I said, "Is this granddaughter the child of your son or your daughter?"

"She is the child of my daughter," she answered, still quietly, still half looking, but not smiling. "But my daughter died ten years ago. Of stomach cancer."

I waited a moment, took a breath, and said, "Was that the worst thing that ever happened to you?"

She thought for a little bit and then said, "No. I think it was my first husband's death that was the worst thing that ever happened to me."

I waited again, wondering what to say next, caught up short not so much by the pain in her life as by her capacity to reflect about degrees of worse. Then the conversation seemed to pick up by itself. Her second husband had also died. Her first child, a son, had been stillborn. A second son had died after Vietnam, "something to do with Agent Orange," she thought. One daughter was still living. She had three great-grandchildren in West Virginia. Her voice was modulated, her story straightforward. The remembering aloud of the major grief of a lifetime—in five minutes, to a stranger—seemed remarkable in its ordinariness.

I said, "Are you a religious woman?"

She looked up, turned straight to me for the first time, and smiled. "I do the best I can," she said.

"Does your church hold you up?" I asked.

"It does. But you know what? I have very good neighbors. I talk to my neighbors."

Her grandson returned with apologies about the line being too long at the concession stand to get a Pepsi and the news that their flight was boarding. As I watched them leave, I looked around the boarding lounge at everyone else coming and going and thought about how heroic people are, everyone walking around in the middle of their whole personal life of suffering and happiness, doing the best they can. I thought about how good people are, about how kind it was to have a stranger, a momentary neighbor, make the story of her life into a teaching story for me and then, just by getting up and keeping going, reminding me that we have Energy enough, and heart enough, for the whole trip.

"YOU'RE NOT GOING TO GET TO DO TODAY OVER": EVERYDAY ENERGY PRACTICE

The one rebuke I recall ever hearing from my mother made a huge impression on me. I was fourteen years old. I was, for whatever reason—I'd like to think adolescent hormones—having a bad day and letting my family know I was unhappy in ways which included banging doors shut behind me as I moved around at home. I remember exactly which door I'd just banged when my mother looked up and said, "You know, Sylvia, you're not going to get to do today over." Poof! All the steam went out of my door-slamming mood. I know that what I experienced, most of all, was surprise. Not because of the rebuke, which was mild enough. It was the news. It *was* the only day that was going to be *that* day.

Thirty years later, my teacher Joseph Goldstein, in a retreat interview in which I reported to him about my practice, offered me the only "rebuke" of our long relationship. (I don't remember what I was doing. Probably speculating or dreaming up philosophical theories.)

Joseph said, "Don't do that, Sylvia. You've been practicing hard. Your attention is good. Use it to pay *closer* attention. You have a lot of Energy available to you. Don't
squander it!"

The urgency of the task—it's painful to suffer, and
there is so little time to undo a lifetime, maybe more, of
habits of suffering!—is a compelling call to pay attention
all the time, not letting the mind be seduced into day-
dreams. Here are questions you could ask yourself during the day, on a bus, at work, at home looking out the
window: "What's going on here that I don't see?" "What
am I missing?" "What *could* I be seeing that would open
my heart or lift it up?" You could think of it as con-
templation practice, reflecting on the present moment,
expecting to learn something new. The expectation energizes attention.

CHAPTER SIX

Patience

////////////////////////

The Buddha, in a prior incarnation as a jungle buffalo, was tick-led and teased by a mischievous monkey but remained steadfast in his Patience. A forest sprite chided him, urging him to frighten the monkey with his considerable strength. The buffalo resists: "I'll upset my own heart," he says. He tells the sprite that a more short-tempered being, one who responded to teasing with anger, might hurt the monkey. He says that the monkey might not have a friend.

The monkey, overhearing the buffalo's concern, comes down from his hiding place in the trees and thanks the buffalo for being such a good friend.

The monkey and the forest sprite each commit themselves to the Magic Charm of Patience.

—A JATAKA TALE

PATIENCE

The practice of:	Develops the habit of:	By:	And is supported by:	And manifests as:
Patience	Abiding	Understanding "This will change" and "It cannot be other, yet" (insight into impermanence, and into karma)	Cultivating tranquillity by practicing Wise Concentration (the mind-steadying aspect of the Eightfold Path, the Fourth Noble Truth)	Tolerance

Since Patience, by definition, can only be present in response to a visiting stress, perfecting Patience depends on being able to feel at home, to relax in the middle of the tension of waiting for the stress to be gone. Patience remains present as long as the mind remembers that things end ("This stress *will* leave, sometime") when their conditioning causes end ("I am not in charge"). Wise Concentration keeps the mind tranquil and the body comfortable so that Patience can keep itself from running out.

PATIENCE MEDITATION

In a Gahan Wilson cartoon in *The New Yorker,* a line of men in Zen robes are seated in classic cross-legged meditation posture and each of them, except for one, has his eyes closed, his body erect, his hands folded in his lap. The remaining meditator is hunched slightly forward, cupping his mouth with his hand and speaking conspiratorially into his cell phone. He is saying, "None of this seems to be doing me any good at all."

I think it's the cell phone that makes the cartoon funny. We laugh at what we recognize as resistance to waiting. If the same caption were drawn into a thought bubble over the man's head, it would be an illustration of the legitimate question "What good is meant to come out of meditation?" The fact that the meditator is phoning in public space in the middle of a meditation session rather than in the privacy of his room suggests that the discomfort in his mind about not knowing the answer has exceeded the decorum demands of the situation. He can't wait.

Even now, as you read these instructions, possibly

anticipating that I'll say, "Please put down the book and close your eyes," you may have the thought "What good is five minutes—even ten—of eyes closed, doing nothing?" Here's a clue: Don't think of it as doing nothing. Think of it as practicing abiding in the moment, as developing Patience. Think of it as a time for discovering that each new moment of experience is related to the previous one, contingent on it but different. Think about it as an opportunity to test the Second Noble Truth, "Wanting other than what's happening is suffering." Think about it as providing proof of the Third Noble Truth, "Peace is possible, right now, whatever the circumstances." Think about it as demonstrating how experiences unfold on their own when everything that needed to happen before has happened. The hundredth breath you take from now cannot happen before the ninety-ninth. Five minutes cannot happen before four minutes pass. But the breaths will happen and the minutes will pass in due time, just as our lives will. We could choose not to hurry, not to miss this moment, not to miss our lives. We could abide.

Please do close your eyes now and enjoy feeling each breath arrive as the life-giving gift of this moment. Sit five minutes. Maybe even ten.

Pay Attention, for Goodness' Sake

THINKING IT OVER

In 1993 the Dalai Lama taught a weeklong seminar on Patience at the Sheraton Hotel in Tucson, Arizona. His text for the entire week was Chapter 6, "Patience," of *A Guide to the Bodhisattva's Way of Life,* written by the sixth-century Buddhist commentator Shantideva. It has 134 verses. The Dalai Lama read the verses, one by one, in Tibetan and then commented in Tibetan. The translator then repeated the teaching in English. The whole room was an ongoing study in Patience.

Twelve hundred people had registered in advance for the seminar, and they filled the Sheraton. The high level of security that was in place because the Dalai Lama is a head of state required that everyone wear a photo ID badge and wait in line, before every session, to file into the auditorium past the guards standing at the doors. Since everyone had an assigned seat, it took extra time for people to locate their proper spot. No one fussed about the logistics. Each teaching, morning and afternoon, was two hours long. Once the Dalai Lama entered, anyone who left could not reenter the room. I never saw anyone leave. No one spoke. It felt like a giant retreat. Everyone seemed to hang on every word, including the long stretches in Tibetan.

〜〜〜〜

Chapter 6 of Shantideva's text describes one situation after another in which the mind might become impatient, angry at what is happening and poised to strike back. Each hypothetical situation, "What if it happened that..." or "What if someone..." is followed by instructions for reinterpreting the situation so that what was felt as abuse becomes a cause for establishing wisdom, gathering the merit of developing Patience, and ensuring continued equanimity. It's amazing. The list of what-if situations includes "What if someone hurts you with a weapon?" "What if someone says bad things about you, especially untrue bad things, possibly jeopardizing your reputation?" "What if you are obligated to care for a relative, one who has many needs, one who could be responsible for his or her own livelihood?" The one about defaming one's reputation is my favorite. I can hear my mind sputtering its protest, "But that's not *true!* But... But..."

I'll use those three situations to show you Shantideva's instructions for keeping the mind relaxed, even benevolent, for maintaining Patience. *A Guide to the Bodhisattva's Way of Life* is in verse form, not prose, and the responses don't really begin with the words "Wait. Think it over," but they imply them.

What if someone hurts you with a weapon? Wait.

Think it over. You probably feel angry. That's normal. But wasn't it the stick striking your body that hurt you? Can you be angry at the stick? Of course not. Should you be angry at the wielder of the stick? Wouldn't it make more sense to be angry at the hatred in the mind of the stick wielder? If you think about it, isn't the end of hatred in the world what you want most of all? Why, then, would you add to it by giving energy to your anger? After all, it will pass on its own if left alone, especially if you respond to it with compassion.

What if a relative, able to be responsible for her own support, relies on you for her care? You might think, Shantideva says, that you are being unjustly exploited, and feel angry. But wait. Think it over. Isn't what you want most the awakening of all beings? If in your heart you truly want this enormous boon for all beings, surely you wouldn't begrudge them the much smaller favor of caring for their daily needs. And anyway, do you really want to be thinking envious thoughts like "She is getting to have everything done for her and I'm needing to work so hard"? Do you think that's good for your own awakening?

Now, my favorite. What if someone says something unfavorable about you? You'll surely feel indignant. But wait. Think it over. Does indignation feel good? No. Does it cloud the mind? Yes. And what if the unfavorable thing the person said was true? Might you not learn something important about yourself, something you are glad to know about, something you could change? Wouldn't that person become your benefactor? And suppose that what the person said about you wasn't true. If it's not true, you *could* just leave it alone. It's just words.

It's wonderful, isn't it? It makes such good sense. Stop. Wait. Think it over. There must be *some* way to not disturb the peace in your heart and add more upset to the world.

For the whole week in Tucson, the Dalai Lama read the verses and commented and we all listened. On the last day, as he was coming up to the final verse, he suddenly hunched forward and held his head in his hands. No one moved. The room was silent. I had the alarmed thought "Maybe he's taken ill!" Then, after some minutes during which everyone sat quite still, the Dalai Lama lifted his head. He was crying. He had become overwhelmed, apparently, by the enormous power of the message of absolute commitment to maintaining a peaceful, benevolent heart. The chapter does not build to a climax. It is one long clarion call for Patience. The first verse is the same as the last. Do *not* give way to impatience. It's not good for you. It's not good for anyone.

And it wasn't as if the Dalai Lama were reading Shantideva's teaching on Patience for the first time. He had surely given that teaching—"Do *not* give in to anger"—many, many times before. The message clearly had not gotten any less powerful for him. I felt the power of that message in the riveted, patient attention of the twelve hundred people in the room and in all of the Dalai Lama's teaching, especially his tears.

THINKING IT OVER FOR A LONG TIME

Once I kept a grudge going for ten years. Someone I knew, a professional colleague, wrote me a letter—a "feedback" letter—telling me what he thought about something I'd done. I hadn't solicited his opinion. It wasn't a complimentary letter. I was enraged. Since I am mild-mannered by nature, rage is not familiar to me, and so I was doubly upset. I was mad at having been maligned, even though it was in the privacy of a letter. And I was mad about feeling so disturbed. I tried not to think about the insult, but it filled my mind. I never looked at the letter again, but I remembered what it said. Each time it came to mind, I thought, *"How* could he have said that about me?"

I didn't tell anyone about the letter, and as time passed, my distress subsided. It came back, though, on those occasions when I knew I'd be meeting this colleague at a conference, even sharing a speaker's podium. Then I would think, *"How* could he have said that about me?" and I'd feel upset again.

I recall telling one of my close friends. We had been talking about the Buddhist practice of Lovingkindness, universal benevolence, and specifically about the four categories of persons—dearly beloved people, good friends, neutral people, and enemies—that we use to identify the people we know. We were imagining those categories as concentric circles of people with ourselves in the middle. "Enemies," people we were mad at, were in the orbit farthest from our heart. We talked about the hoped-for goal that all orbits could disappear and everyone would become equally dear.

"Do you have any enemies?" my friend asked. "Anyone that you've put out of your heart?"

"Only one," I said, and I told her about the letter. I remember saying, "I can't *believe* he said that about me."

"If you have only one name on your enemy list," my friend said, "don't you wish you could erase it?"

"I *do* wish that," I said. "Or at least I think I do. I even feel a little bit embarrassed now, having told you. It seems silly. It was just a letter. And it was a long time ago. But so far I can't let go of it. Thinking about it still riles me. It's too painful. Maybe someday . . ."

One evening I was driving to a meeting where I was to be one of the speakers. I was feeling relaxed and at ease, looking forward to the event, when I realized I would be sharing the program with my "enemy." I thought my reflexive thought, "*How* could he have said that about me?" And then I thought, "Because it's *true!*"

At the meeting we exchanged greetings. We'd done that much many times before. We are both polite people. On that occasion I said, "I'm really glad to see you."

He said, "Me too."

At the end of the evening, he said, "Can we have lunch?"

I said, "I'd like that."

We met for lunch, once a month, for several months. We talked about spiritual practice. We talked about our lives. We ended each lunch by saying, "I'm so glad we're doing this," but neither of us brought up the ten-year hiatus in our friendship. Finally I did.

I said, "I want to tell you what happened to me when I got your letter." I told the whole story, just as I've told it here, and ended by saying, "When I greeted you so wholeheartedly that evening, I was feeling wonderful because it was such a relief to stop hiding from myself. When I asked myself, '*How* could he have said that about me?' I realized that you said it because it's true."

And he said, "No, it's not."

Then he told me his story, particularly how embarrassed he had felt about having written impulsively. He told me stories from his life, stories that explained why this particular act of impulsiveness had felt so painful to him. We both felt pained for each other.

"You were right, though," I said, "about what you said about me. I *had* made the wrong decision you said I made. I was covering it up for myself so that I wouldn't see it, so I wouldn't need to acknowledge it or deal with it. Your letter gave me the chance to avoid dealing with it for ten years. I could just be mad at your harsh words or at you and not look at my own stuff. I realized that my decision was a wrong one years ago, and I amended it. I think I forgot to notice, by then, that I'd felt ashamed and been mad at *myself* all along, not at you. I'm sorry I waited so long. Thanks for waiting for me."

"Me too," he said. "Thanks for waiting."

It's been some years now, and our relationship has continued to blossom. Sometimes I even tell this story with him in the audience. No one knows who the person is—"he" might even become a "she"—since I am eager to protect our privacy. And sometimes people ask, "Why did you both wait so long?" "Don't you both have better communication skills?" "Aren't you sad about the ten years?" And I say, "Being sad now about a time that's past would mean extra pain. I'm happy now." And "We do have better communication skills than that story might suggest. We had the skills then too. They just weren't up and running. We were both too confused by pain." And "We're patient people. It just took that long for our minds to clear."

I don't know why everything changed on the day that it did. If I were telling the grudge story as an explanation of karma, how cause-and-effect interrelatedness works, I might say, "The necessary and sufficient conditions for change to happen were finally present." In this case, I think the condition was Patience—which necessarily takes time—to see what *really* was making me mad.

UNGLAMOROUS COURAGE

My friend Mary calls Patience "unglamorous courage." It's noticed mainly in its absence. It doesn't seem heroic, like signing up for assignments that merit hazard pay, although both require the same sense that "this needs to get done." Neither is it necessarily stalwart, like Dr. Seuss's Horton the Elephant, who "meant what he said and said what he meant," was "faithful one hundred percent," and sat on a nest to hatch an egg for a "good-for-nothing" bird. Horton, sitting through ice storms, looks more long-suffering than patient to me. He is gritting his teeth. Patience is more the quiet moment-to-moment adjustment to unpleasant circumstances done in the knowledge that they cannot be other. It is Wisdom.

Patience depends on remembering that everything is always changing, so the current, unavoidable challenge will eventually end. Children traveling in the backseat on long car trips ask, "Are we there yet?" when it's clear to them that they aren't, and "How many more minutes?" at a time when it doesn't seem helpful to be asking. After all, if five minutes previously the answer was "Fifty-five more minutes" and the response now is "Fifty more minutes," it still is a long drive. What I think happens, though, is that the reminder that time *does* pass is reassuring.

At any age, the ability to wait calmly depends on how desirable we imagine the goal of the waiting to be and how reasonable the period of discomfort seems. My sense is that it is harder to keep Patience going for thirty minutes in the Department of Motor Vehicles than it is for the entire last trimester of a pregnancy. A woman who is happily looking forward to delivering a healthy baby doesn't *want* to have the child early. If her health is good and her baby's health seems fine, she waddles through the last weeks before the due date joking about how hard it is to move around. The good mood is harder to sustain if the child's birth is delayed, even a little: "It should have arrived four *days* ago!" Of course, it shouldn't arrive until the very best time for it to arrive, but to the mind that has kept itself balanced by planning on a particular time, extra waiting, "when it isn't necessary," feels tedious.

My friend Meg, who died after an intense eleven-year effort to overcome ovarian cancer, relied on being able after her first surgery, then after her second surgery, then through the five days following each of her thirty-four rounds of chemotherapy when she was so terribly sick, to project her attention forward to the time when she would resume her life with her partner, her painting, her poetry. She definitely did not feel heroic. "I am terrified," she said, "each time I find myself walking into the hospital for the chemo. It's bizarre to know I am about to voluntarily put poison in my body. I know I'm about to feel awful for five days. But what's my alternative? I want to live. I've had a remission. I could have another. In between, my life is good."

Meg did her dying patiently as well. The whole process, from the time her doctors said, "Nothing is working anymore. We need to stop. Your body will wind down in its own natural rhythm," to the time Meg died quietly, at home, in her sleep, took five months. The doctors had guessed that the time would be shorter. Meg got weaker and weaker, and after one last evening out with friends, celebrating her partner's birthday at their favorite restaurant, she stayed at home. "I'll do this as a retreat," she said. "It will be over when it's over."

Her pain got worse. She took morphine. "I don't want to take more than I need," she said. "I don't want to be foggy-minded if I don't have to be. But I don't need to be a hero about it either. If I hurt, I'll take it. I don't think you get extra points for suffering."

In the days just before she died, Meg slept a lot. The last time I visited she said, "I sleep really deeply. When I wake up, I feel that I've been gone so long. I don't know how long I've slept—maybe it's just been a few minutes—but it feels like I've come back a great distance to wake up here again. Death is so mysterious."

"What do you mean, mysterious?" I asked.

"Oh," Meg said, smiling at me. "Were you thinking I meant mysterious as in those stories about seeing the light or seeing people on the other side?"

"I suppose I was," I said. "Do you see anything while you're gone?"

"No," Meg answered. "I don't see anything at all. I just sleep deeply. I meant it's mysterious in how long it takes. I'm always a little surprised that I'm back. I guess it will just happen when it happens."

THE ENDLESS ROPE

We use odd expressions to talk about patience that make it sound like a quantifiable, storable commodity like olive oil, gasoline, or money in the bank: "I'm getting low on patience." "My patience is coming to an end." "I am about to run out of patience." The French say, *"Je suis au bout de ma force"* (I am at the end of my strength). We say, "I am at the end of my rope."

I don't think we have an internal reservoir in which we store up Patience for a time when we'll need it. I think it's more like the energy-saving water heater I have at my house. There is no holding tank of hot water. The heater clicks on when I turn the hot water tap on, and the cold water flowing through it gets heated en route to the shower. It keeps on heating water as long as I'm using it, and then it clicks off again.

I don't need hot water in the middle of the night while I'm sleeping, and I don't need Patience then, either.

I do need Patience whenever the demands of the moment are overwhelming my capacity to handle them easily. If I am in a sustained amount of pain in my mind or in my body—too tired, too worried, too sad, too confused—I become frightened and feel impatient for my situation to end. If I remind myself, "This *will* end. There *is* nothing I can do. I *am* uncomfortable, but I can, at least, be kind to myself in my discomfort," I feel better. I relax. My Patience is restored. The rope that I thought I was at the end of disappears. It turns out to be imaginary. The kindness, though, is not imaginary. It makes a difference. The kindness steadies the mind. And in circumstances of high vigilance, which is what moments of impatience are, the possibility exists—if the mind is balanced—for learning something new.

I invited Art George, a driving safety teacher in Marin County, California, to meet me for tea because a friend of mine who took his class so she could clear her record of a speeding ticket said, "You'll like him, Sylvia. He teaches Mindfulness." Spirit Rock Meditation

Center—where I teach Mindfulness—is also in Marin County, and Art laughed when I phoned to invite him and told him my friend's observation. When we met I said, "What did she mean?"

He said, "Well, I often begin the first class by telling the same story. I'll tell it to you." This is Art's story:

I was driving north on Highway 101, just ten minutes past the Golden Gate Bridge, on my way to the Richmond Bridge in San Rafael. I planned to cross the bay and drive on north from there to Antioch, where I had an important business meeting. Even though it was midday, I found myself suddenly in gridlock traffic. I thought I might miss my appointment in Antioch. I began to feel anxious. I became irritated at the drivers ahead of me jockeying between lanes. Then I became irritated at the drivers I saw joining the freeway traffic from entrance ramps without leaving any space for the cars already on the highway to move forward. It was looking less and less likely that I'd be at my appointment on time. I noticed that my body had become tense and I was gripping the wheel. Then I looked out the driver's side window and saw Mount Tamalpais. I looked out to my right and saw Richardson Bay. I thought, "I am sitting between two major tourist attractions. People come from all over the world to sit exactly where I am sitting right now in order to have this view." I sat back and appreciated the view. My hands unclenched. My body relaxed. My *mind* relaxed. Then I had this big revelation.

Art stopped his narrative, then leaned forward to tell me the end of his story.

This was my revelation: "I'll get to Antioch when I get to Antioch. Maybe today. Maybe not today. Maybe I'll be there for the meeting. Maybe I won't be there for the meeting. Whatever will be will be. My getting aggravated is not changing the situation. It is making it worse."

I applauded his story. I said, "You really *are* a Mindfulness teacher."

He said, "I'm not finished. I always go on to tell the class that when the traffic did start up again, I didn't drive too fast, so I didn't become a menace to myself and everyone else on the highway. That's the important part. I say to my students, 'You need to keep looking for whatever perspective you can find that will transform the moment.'"

Then he said, "You might be thinking, what if people ask me what I would do if I wasn't between Mount Tamalpais and Richardson Bay? I might, for example, be stuck in traffic on the Pulaski Skyway between Newark and Jersey City, where it's extremely polluted and also crowded. I tell people, 'You can look out of a window *anywhere*. On the Pulaski Skyway you could say to yourself, 'Look at this wonderful ironwork that they made a hundred years ago. They don't do ironwork like this anymore.' Maybe if your spirits are a little bit lifted by admiring the craftsmanship, you'll have the courage to look at the pollution on the Pulaski Skyway and say, 'It's really polluted here. I wonder what technology people will develop in the twenty-first century to clean it up. I wonder what I could do to help. I wonder whom I could call in Congress, whom I might help elect that might have some impact on this situation.' I tell people," Art said, "that the main thing about being a safe driver is looking out for other people. Not just on the road. All the time."

"ALWAYS? *REALLY?*":
EVERYDAY PATIENCE PRACTICE

No one needs to especially devise situations in which to cultivate Patience. They present themselves freely. The bus is late. It's crowded. The person boarding in front of you does not have exact change. You know, because you checked at home before you left, that the e-mail you were expecting has not arrived, and you are eager to get to work so that you can check again. The bus is moving slowly. The living of regular, ordinary everyday life—even when it is most simple—requires ongoing attention to diffusing *im*patience.

I often use humor to cultivate Patience. I like jokes, so I sweeten my mind by mock editing on the margins of my thoughts. "This bus is *always* late." "Always? *Really?*" "It's too crowded." "Too crowded for what?" "This person should have had exact change ready." "Why?" "In a million years that e-mail won't be there!" "In a million years the e-mail *will* be there. Probably by this afternoon." If I'm funny enough, I'll laugh at myself for rushing around through my life creating schedules that I feel bound to meet, forgetting that I am in competition with the rest of the world unfolding on its own time line. I'll relax, I'll be patient,

I'll probably look around at the people sharing my situation.

That's the everyday Patience practice: cheering the mind. Your technique will be uniquely yours. Perhaps you sing to yourself or recite long poems you know by heart. The mind, cheered up, remembers that it is worrying that things won't turn out well because they aren't happening "on time" and that the current discomfort will never end. It also remembers that "on time" is an idea we've made up so our calendars work, and that the discomfort will end. Everything ends.

CHAPTER SEVEN

Truthfulness

///////////////////////////

A wise person, upon acknowledging the truth,
becomes like a lake;
clear and deep and still.
Find friends who love the truth.
—THE BUDDHA

TRUTHFULNESS

The practice of:	Develops the habit of:	By:	And is supported by:	And manifests as:
Truthfulness	Disclosing	Discovering what is true, and telling the truth in ways that are helpful (practicing Wise Mindfulness and Wise Speech, the mind-clarifying and speech-guiding aspects of the Fourth Noble Truth)	Experiencing the discomforting isolation of guile (separation from self and others) and the ease (and peace) of candor (the Third Noble Truth)	Intimacy

To perfect my Truthfulness I need to be able to tolerate seeing clearly all of who I am and all of what is happening. I need to not feel ashamed or afraid. If I pay attention calmly and steadily, my mind will be unbiased and its secrets will reveal themselves to me in an honest, gentle way. I will not be distressed. The pleasure I'll experience by not hiding from myself will inspire me to create the intimacy of nonjudgmental, gentle honesty with everyone.

TRUTHFULNESS MEDITATION

Sgt. Joe Friday, the detective hero of the TV crime drama *Dragnet,* would stop witnesses in midsentence if he thought their testimony was opinion. "Just the facts, ma'am," he would say. "Just give me the facts." Sgt. Friday's signature phrase became the culturally understood equivalent of "Get to the point, please. What is the heart of this matter? What are you trying to say? What are you hiding from me—or from yourself—in this smoke screen of extra embellishment? This is a story! What is the *truth*?" Joe Friday would have made a good Mindfulness teacher.

The Buddha taught that bare attention, impartial, sincere interest without additional commentary, noticing things just as they are, primes the mind for the liberating insight: "There is no one and no thing separate from the continuously unfolding, remarkably lawful, interdependent unfolding of life."

He saw that it was the additional personalized editorializing—"Why me?" "Why not me? "Poor me!"—

that continuously creates a "Me" to whom life is happening, a "Me" bound to suffer.

In the Foundations of Mindfulness Sermon, the Buddha gives meditation instructions for seeing things truly, just as they are. He advises sitting cross-legged, with back erect, at the foot of a tree in the forest or in an empty room, and "establishing oneself in Mindfulness." "Breathing in, one is aware of breathing in. Breathing out, one is aware of breathing out. Breathing in a long breath, one knows, 'I am breathing in a long breath.' Breathing out a long breath, one is aware, 'I am breathing out a long breath.' Breathing in a short breath, one knows, 'I am breathing in a short breath.' Breathing out a short breath, one is aware, 'I am breathing out a short breath.'"

I understand those instructions to mean that if you can see clearly enough to distinguish things by name, you won't be confused by illusion. So here are the Buddha's instructions for radical truth telling, for seeing things as they are: Sit with your body in a posture that is both dignified and relaxed, so that you stay alert and comfortable, and let your attention rest in the sensations of your body. Tell yourself, in words, what's happening. Tell yourself what's true about your body, about your breath, about your mood, about your thoughts. "This is

happening." "Now that is happening." "Now this is happening."

When you practice this truth-telling meditation in a
sitting position, you can close your eyes. If you decide to
practice it as a walking meditation, you'll of course keep
your eyes open. The instruction for naming, for telling
yourself what is happening, remains the same. Tell the
truth. And remember, no stories. Just the facts.

TRUTHFUL AND HELPFUL

The Buddha's criteria for Wise Speech include—in addition to the obvious expectation that speech be truthful—
that it be timely, gentle, motivated by kindness, and
helpful. I've come to think of those five guidelines as
being just two, truthful and helpful. I often teach
Truthfulness as a synonym for Mindfulness, for paying
complete attention, for not hiding from *anything* even if
the acknowledging of it is unpleasant. It's hard to do. In
the middle of the night at a long-ago retreat, an anony-
mous meditator—clearly pained by some personal realization—wrote, in big letters, on the blackboard in front
of the schoolroom we were using for a meditation room,
"All insights are bad news!" I think what that person
meant was, "I wasn't ready to hear that." I think it's

likely that meditator wasn't calm enough, or was too sleepy, to receive the new understanding. Perhaps the tone of voice in which the insight had announced itself had been harsh. Truth that is told gently, with kind intent, when it is genuinely invited—whether we tell it to ourselves or have it told to us—prepares the way in which it can be heard. Then it becomes helpful.

Bill Kwong is the *roshi* (senior teacher) at Sonoma Mountain Zen Center, and in the early years of my meditation practice he was the guest teacher for one afternoon at a retreat at which I was a student. He sat up in front, led a period of formal meditation, and then said, "It's not my custom to give a structured talk. I'd prefer to answer the questions that anyone here might have." At first, people asked him Zen meditation questions: "What is *kensho*?" "What is satori?" "What is enlightenment?" Kwong Roshi responded to each question thoughtfully.

Then somebody said, "I heard you had cancer. How was that?" One of my friends had told me that Bill had been sick, that he'd been treated for cancer, that he'd been pronounced cured of it, but still I thought, "Oh dear, that is *personal!* I thought people were going to ask him *practice* questions!" Bill thought for a while. I held my breath. Then he said, "It was terrible. It was *really* terrible." Straightforward, clear, without drama—honest. Just like that. Then he said a bit more about his experience, about the treatments he'd had, about how glad he was to be better.

It was such a relief to me that he *didn't* say, "My deep realization that all things come and go—including health and life—allowed me to rise above the discomfort of my experience and see it as a passing, empty phenomenon." He said, "It was terrible. It was *really* terrible."

I had realized in the space of Bill's pause before answering that the personal question is the most important practice question. "How are you dealing with the pain in *your* life? In the lives around you? Are you acknowledging it? Telling the truth? Responding with compassion?" "Please tell me the *most* challenging thing that ever happened to you." All these are variations of the question of the student who mentioned Kwong Roshi's cancer and said, "How was that?"

And I realize now that Kwong Roshi's answer, specific to his own situation, is the answer we could all give to the question "How was your greatest challenge?" "It was terrible. It was *really* terrible." The second half of the answer, the line he did not say, the line we understood from his direct, gentle, kind, and truthful response, was "And it was manageable." It is basic Dharma, basic truth, and very helpful.

Truthfulness

NOW AND ZEN

A traditional Zen teaching story begins with the account of elders in a rural Japanese village bringing a newborn infant to the mountaintop home of the local Zen priest, knocking at the gate, and saying, "The unmarried woman who is this child's mother says that you are the father. You need to take care of it." The priest says, "Is that so?" and accepts the baby. Three years later the elders return, saying, "The real father of the child has returned to the village, confessed, and agreed to marry the mother, and now you need to give the child back to us." The priest says, "Is that so?" and gives them the child.

I appreciate the story more now than when I first heard it. It was told to me as an example of nonattachment, of the priest's capacity to let go of something he could no longer have. I wanted the priest to say, "I raised him! He is mine!" or "You can't do this to me!" or "I feel so terrible about losing this child. How can you do this to me?" or "I worked so hard. I don't deserve this." The story upset me because I thought it meant the priest didn't care about the child, that he was indifferent. I think that my discomfort may have been some alarm on my part about the possibility—in the event that my practice worked and I did change my habits of grasping—that I might become indifferent to my own children. I see now that the story has nothing to do with whether the priest liked the child or didn't, or had enjoyed him or hadn't. He was able to recognize the truth of the current situation—the elders were going to take the child—and whatever had been his experience would remain just as it was.

It's difficult to keep the emotions of the present moment from rewriting history. If we are angry, insulted, or embarrassed, the mind often designates the person (or people) we feel caused our distress as "enemies," and substantiates that label by highlighting past experiences that support such a view. It's probably a reflexive, protective attempt of the psyche to soothe our feelings. It doesn't work, though. A revised history isn't the truth, so it requires constant maintenance to keep it going. And it's painful.

A woman I met recently on the New Englander—the train that begins in New Hampshire and passes through western Massachusetts on its way to Philadelphia—might have, but didn't, rewrite her history. There were very few people on the train when I boarded it in Springfield. I noticed one couple, clearly older than I am by a significant number of years, sitting together in the last row, holding hands.

I immediately imagined a history for them: more than fifty years married, several children, many grandchildren. I noticed, as I settled into a seat some rows before them, that they weren't talking to each other, and I wondered whether when Seymour and I have been together fifty years we too will have run out of things to say.

My habit on long train rides is to get up from my seat periodically and walk back and forth up the length of the car several times, just to stretch. On my second or third stretch break, the woman smiled at me, and I stopped to talk. They were still holding hands.

"Are you going all the way to Philadelphia?" I asked.

"We are," the woman answered.

"Do you live there?" I asked. "Are you going home?"

The man spoke. "No," he said. "We live in New Hampshire. But I need a certain surgery that they do only at one particular hospital in Philadelphia. We're going there."

I thought about how wonderful it was that these two old people, having been together so long, were now able to face old-age challenges together.

"How long have you been married?" I asked. I wanted to give them the pleasure of telling me, and anyway, I wanted to know.

"We're not married," the woman replied. "We just met each other three years ago. We live together."

I tried not to look surprised. Then they both told me their stories. The man told his story first. He had married young. His wife had died seven years previously. They'd had five children. His grandchildren were grown. His children still lived in New Hampshire, but most of his grandchildren lived farther away. Many of them came back every summer for a family reunion.

Then the woman told her story. She said, "I was a bit older when I married than he was. I had four children, right away, each a year apart from the next. My husband and I raised them all," she continued, "and they all got married. And then, after forty-four years—after all that—I came home one day and found a note from my husband that he'd left with another woman. That was three years ago. I was *furious*. Can you imagine?"

I tried to imagine. I thought about two mismatched people struggling through so many years, trying to raise their family.

"It must have been a really bad forty-four years," I ventured—half question, half answer. I mainly was aiming for a sympathetic tone as a response to her disclosure of having been furious.

"Not at *all*," she answered. "It was the best forty-four

years of my life! We had a good time together. We had great children. His business did fine. We all went on holidays together. It was fine. Then he got this nonsense going. . . ." She stopped in midsentence and waved one hand at the wrist as if to brush the story away. "It's all right now," she said. "I run into him all the time. Just this morning we passed him at the train station as we were getting on the train."

Then she asked me why I was going to Philadelphia. "I'm going to teach," I said. I knew she had seen me writing at my seat as she had passed me on her trips through the car. "I write books about having a good attitude, and I'll probably write a story about you."

She looked puzzled. "*What* good attitude?" she said. "I just told you I was furious."

"But you didn't let the furiousness leak out over your whole life," I offered, feeling a bit awkward. I had been trying to compliment her for making a wise choice between two possible attitude options, one skillful and one not, and apparently the unwise one—the one that would not have been truthful or helpful—hadn't even appeared on her radar screen.

"You could have continued to be mad at him," I said, "mad that he left you. You could have resented the forty-four years."

"No, I couldn't," she said. "At the end there, it was rough. But they were the best years of my life. *That's* the truth."

"DON'T KNOW MIND"

Students of the Korean teacher Seung Sahn, the founder of the Providence Zen Center, and students of Kalu Rimpoche, a lama (priest) in the Tibetan Buddhist tradition, arranged for the two venerable lineage holders to appear together for a public dialogue. Seung Sahn took an orange out of the sleeve of his robes, held it up for Kalu Rimpoche to see, and said, in the forthright style characteristic of Zen, "What is *this*?" Kalu Rimpoche's interpreters translated the question for him, but he seemed mystified. "What *is* this?" Seung Sahn repeated the question. Still the lama remained mystified. Seung Sahn asked a third time.

Kalu Rimpoche turned to his interpreter and said, "What's the matter with him? Don't they have oranges in Korea?"

I have a personal connection to that story. When I was a child my father used the time we spent at dinner together to ask me challenging questions. I recall him holding up a grapefruit and saying, "What is this?"

I said, "It's a grapefruit."

He said, "What color is it?"

I said, "It's yellow."

He said, "How do you know?"

"Because it *is* yellow," I said. "Everyone knows that. Don't *you* think it's yellow?"

"I do," he replied. "But how do you know that what I see and call yellow is the same as what *you* see and call yellow?"

I didn't know. But I knew it was a hard question, and I felt proud that he asked me. Now I think of it as an early invitation to tolerate the tension of not knowing *yet,* of wondering. I assume that what Seung Sahn was asking about the orange was, "Can you move past a conventional level of response?"

These days we use the expression "thinking outside the box" to mean including perspectives we hadn't thought of as possible options. We are hoping, when we use that expression, that new understanding will emerge, understanding currently unavailable to us because our view is blocked by an opinion. Seung Sahn used a particular instructional phrase, one often employed to summarize the gist of his teaching, that is the equivalent of "think outside the box." He used to say, "Only keep 'Don't Know Mind'!"

My friend Louise, a professor of sociology at a large university, told me about a dramatic shift in understanding—one that involved letting go of a long-cherished opinion—that happened to her, unexpectedly, at the annual faculty retreat of her departmental colleagues. She said, "This year we invited a psychologist, a communications specialist, to facilitate the meeting. The department has become quite large, and there were some sensitive topics we needed to discuss. We thought an outsider would be able to hold a broad perspective for the discussions." Louise went on to say that it happened that she and the facilitator were seated at the same table in the dining room for all the meals. She had enjoyed their continuing conversations.

"Sunday at lunch," Louise told me, "at our final meal of the weekend, the facilitator said to me, 'I notice you don't eat any cooked vegetables. Why is that?'

"I said, 'When I was a child, my mother forced me to eat cooked vegetables.'"

Louise paused in her story and smiled so that I knew I could anticipate a punch line.

"The facilitator said, 'That was a *long* time ago.'"

We both were touched by the emperor's-new-clothes, stating-what-is-obvious quality of the psychologist's response. We understood that the challenge to reflect upon was not about how much time has elapsed since Louise was a child. We would both acknowledge—and I'm sure the psychologist would, too—that a trauma could take a long time to heal. What had become clear in Louise's mind—and in mine when she told me about it—was that the dislike of cooked vegetables must have *preceded* the forcing. Otherwise, her mother wouldn't have thought she needed to force her. Probably the most accurate answer to the question "Why don't you eat cooked vegetables?" would have been "I don't like them. Never did."

"After that retreat," Louise said, "I decided to let my mother off the hook about the vegetables. I stopped telling people stories about how difficult my mother had been to live with. I stopped telling *myself* those stories. I decided that my mother probably had been worried about my health. I was a skinny kid, sick a lot. My mother probably thought the vegetables had vitamins in them that I needed. My mother *was* pushy," Louise said, making sure I understood that the eating struggles, and other childhood struggles, had been unpleasant for her, "but I think I used that as a cover story. I told people I moved to San Francisco *because* my mother was pushy. The truth is, I moved to San

Francisco because I wanted to live here. My mother was old when I moved, and afraid to have me so far away. I think I felt guilty about leaving her and I didn't want to deal with it."

She thought for a moment. "Moving was the right decision. My job is great. I'm happy here. The story that my mother was difficult wasn't the *whole* truth. I see her more clearly now. I know she's proud of me. And I think she did the best she could. I've even gotten into the habit of calling her every Friday. She looks forward to it. Even *I* look forward to it. I never imagined this would happen. As long as I couldn't tell the truth, we *both* suffered. Now we don't."

"TELL THE TRUTH, BE YOURSELF, YOU'LL BE FINE": EVERYDAY TRUTHFULNESS PRACTICE

When I feel loved and loving, I am protected and my speech is protected. I can say what I feel is true. I can teach forthrightly. I can even disagree, confident that I won't do harm. I couldn't deceive or insult people I loved. And if I feel loved, I can't feel ashamed, so I have no need for guile. Being able to tell the truth is a great relief because it doesn't require the prompter in the

mind that says, "Don't say this," "What if they disagree?" "Stop! You'll look foolish." I am free to be myself. Candor thrives in an atmosphere of goodwill. My
everyday truthfulness practice is keeping goodwill alive
in me.

My goodwill—everyone's goodwill—is challenged
by fear. I see most clearly how feeling even a bit tense
begins to compromise my ability to be authentic when I
am about to teach people I don't know. If I pay attention, I'll hear my mind manufacturing doubting, distanc-
ing thoughts: "What if I am not good enough?" "What if
I'm not smart enough?" "What if I'm not spiritual
enough?" and on and on. I'm very good at mushrooming
minor mind wobbles into major worries. If I am paying
enough attention, I'll think: "What's the truth, Sylvia?
The truth is, all these people came here because they expect to be interested. They came as friends. They already like me. I like what I already know, and I'm not
going to get any smarter, or any more spiritual, in the
next two minutes." Then I look around the room. I
smile. I say to the people there—silently, so they don't
hear me—"I love you!" I often hear my friend Jonathan's
voice saying what I long ago deputized him to say to me
in other, similar situations: "Be yourself. Tell the truth.
You'll be fine."

So the instruction for everyday Truthfulness practice has two parts. First, do whatever you find works for you to counteract anxiety. Then, with natural goodwill firmly in place, tell the truth, be yourself, and you'll be fine.

CHAPTER EIGHT

Determination

////////////

The Monkey Who Would Not Give Up

The Buddha, in a prior incarnation as the chief of a band of monkeys, steadfastly protected his tribe from being discovered, and harmed, by the people who lived downstream on the Ganges from the huge and wonderful mango tree in which they lived.

One day, a mango fell from the tree and was carried by the river to the bathing site of King Brahmadatta, who, enchanted by the taste of the fruit, traveled with a search party and found the tree. The monkeys overheard the men planning to kill them and eat their meat as well as the mangoes. They were terrified.

The chief of the monkeys, determined to save them, tied a reed to his foot, leapt across the river, and barely managed to grasp a branch on the other side. "Run across the reed," he called, "and over my back." Eighty thousand monkeys ran to safety.

The monkey chief's back was broken. King Brahmadatta held him as he died, and asked who he was. The monkey said: "I am their king and I loved them. I do not suffer since, by my death, my subjects are free. Remember, it is not your sword that makes you king; it is love alone." Thereafter, Brahmadatta ruled with love and his people were happy ever after.

—*A* JATAKA *TALE*

DETERMINATION

The practice of:	Develops the habit of:	By:	And is supported by:	And manifests as:
Determination	Persevering	Seeing clearly into the cause of suffering so that the resolve to change habits of mind becomes spontaneous (practicing Wise Understanding and Wise Intention, the mind-energizing aspects of the Fourth Noble Truth)	Validating, through direct experience, the possibility of a peaceful mind (the Third Noble Truth) and consolidating, through repeated experience, the spiritual faculty of faith	Tenacity

Each time I feel the pain of being "reborn into suffering" through inattention, by falling prey to lust or being overwhelmed by anger, I am reinspired in my Determination to dismantle the obstacle course of confusion that seems to trip my mind at every turn. Each time I stay successfully balanced, each time I recognize that hurdles of temptation are startling—but not substantial—I become more confirmed in my faith. Peace *is* possible, and I can experience it. Perseverance, the hallmark of Determination, becomes automatic.

DETERMINATION MEDITATION

I saw a greeting card—probably in the section of the card rack labeled "Humorous: Over Sixty"—that read, "Finally I got it all together, and then I forgot where I put it." I thought, "It doesn't *matter* if you forget. What matters is that you remember that 'getting it together' is a possibility." Near that card—in the "Spiritual Sentiments" section—was another card, quoting the poet Robert Frost: "First thing I do in the morning is I make up my bed. Then I make up my mind." I liked the second card better. It addressed the same issue—the need to recover something lost—but it didn't sound disappointed. It sounded normal, resolute, *determined*.

Beds—and minds—get rumpled. It's the same rumple, over and over, requiring the same straightening, day after day. Tidying up—beds and minds—reveals lost car keys and lost insights. Perseverance in tidying depends on faith: "I've seen it before. I *know* it's in here some-where."

Think for a moment now about what—in your whole life—was your clearest experience of the Buddha's Third Noble Truth, "The end of suffering is possible. Peace is possible." Take your time. Probably more than one experience comes to mind. You want to take enough time to feel each of those experiences with the whole of your body as the memory appears in your mind. Maybe you can taste the experience. Or hear it. Or smell it. It might be an experience of exquisite seren-ity—one in which the truths of your own life and of the world, with sorrows as well as joys—are acknowledged with ease and steadfastness of heart. Or it might be an experience of such overwhelming happiness that all awareness of sorrow vanishes in a mind of limitless grat-itude.

Whatever in you found a memory and felt it—or even almost found or felt a memory—is the place in you that already knows that peace is possible. Peace is possible in the middle of this life, in this very body, in these very relationships, in this very world. Remembering that we already know that peaceful appreciation is the natural response of the heart when the mind is relaxed and attentive invites us to straighten up our minds yet again. Remembering lets us come back home and find once more what we're looking for.

Now straighten the mind with your breath. Bring your attention to your plain, ordinary breathing, one breath after another. Try to sustain an interest in each breath, the tenth as well as the first. The practice of sustaining keeps the attention from wobbling. Sustaining is the antidote to doubt. And the absence of doubt reveals the presence of faith. You've already confirmed that you have faith. Peace *is* possible. Now just live it. Breathe.

ACT OF FAITH

Sometimes I sit down on my meditation cushion and say to myself, "I'm not getting up until I'm enlightened." When I say that in class my students often laugh, because they know the story of the Buddha who, twenty-five hundred years ago, was said to have made a similar statement of Determination as he sat down under the bodhi tree in Bodh Gaya on the eve of his enlightenment. They also know that, according to legend, he had, in countless previous lifetimes, fully developed all of the Paramitas—and they know I haven't. I interpret their laughter as meaning, "Do you *really* think you'll become enlightened in that very sitting?" And I say, "It's a faith statement. I too am thinking about the Buddha. I am remembering that seeing clearly, choosing wisely, and loving fully is a human possibility. Why *shouldn't* I say that to myself?"

I often then tell them the story that my teacher, colleague, and friend Sharon Salzberg tells about going to Asia to study Lovingkindness practice with the venerable Burmese meditation teacher Sayadow U Pandita. At her first interview with him, U Pandita asked, "How do you think you are going to do with this practice?" Sharon thought, "Probably this is a trick question to see if I have too much pride." So she said, "Really, I don't know. Maybe I'll do well, but maybe I won't do well."

U Pandita said, "That's not a helpful way to think. Think instead, 'I'm going to do great. I'm going to do wonderfully at this.'"

Of course—why not? It's much more energizing to think positively. Whenever I've said, "I'm not getting up until I'm enlightened," I haven't said it frivolously. Nor have I thought of it as an announcement of a definite result. I usually say it in times of dismay and confusion. My declaration mobilizes my faith. I remember, in those moments, the stories of great numbers of people who, while listening to the Buddha preach, were so eager to free their minds that in one sudden moment of understanding—or grace—they became enlightened. Greed and hatred and delusion never arose in them again. I think of the descriptions of those experiences and the classic line used to explain them, "And their hearts, through not clinging, were liberated from taints," and I feel—without any question about results—absolute resolve. I sit down determined.

And it always works. Dismay and confusion disappear. Not forever, but long enough for the mind to steady itself and for my faith to be restored. It isn't magic that clears the mind. The very act of Determination, the decisive energy of a moment of absolute resolve, sweeps confusion away and pumps the mind back up to its natural strength. It doesn't matter if it doesn't last forever. That it works is what matters. It builds confidence. We remember, like the Little Engine That Could, that "I think I can, I think I can, I think I can" translates into Determination, success, and such a sure ride home that the next mountain down the road looks more like a hill.

Determination

THE POWERS OF PRACTICE

My grandson Collin's sixth-grade teacher invited me to visit her class and talk to her students about the Buddha and meditation. They were completing a social studies unit on India. I was eager to present Mindfulness as non-mysterious, sensible, and useful because, first of all and most importantly, it is. Also, because I am Collin's grandmother, I wanted to appear "regular."

"Mindfulness is about paying attention," I told them. "Think about how useful it is to be able to concentrate here in class. It's much easier to finish your assignments, isn't it, if you aren't distracted by the people around you?"

I saw that all twenty-six students seemed to be smiling, nodding, agreeing.

"And," I continued, "when we pay attention carefully, we make wise decisions. Do you know what *wise* means?"

More nodding and smiling.

"My grandpa wasn't wise," one girl said. "He kept on smoking cigarettes after he *knew* they were bad for him, and he got sick."

Other students joined in with stories of people they knew who were, or weren't, wise.

"I heard," one boy said politely, "that people who meditate can tell the future, or know your past, or even guess what you're thinking right now."

"That's true," I responded. "Some people do learn that skill by meditating, but Mindfulness is about paying attention."

"I also heard," the same boy continued, "that people who meditate can walk over hot coals or lie on beds of nails. We saw pictures of that in our book about India."

"That's true too," I answered. "Sometimes people concentrate so hard that they don't feel pain in the way we usually do. Then they can do those special things that you saw in your book to prove how concentrated they are. Mindfulness is different. Mindfulness is paying attention in an ordinary way."

"Collin said," he went on, "that you once met a woman who was such a good meditator that she could walk through walls. Did you?"

"I did," I said, laughing, appreciating how polite *and* persistent this young man was in pursuing his point. "She was old when I met her. She lived in Calcutta, but some of her students, who were my teachers, brought her to the United States so people here could meet her."

"Did you talk to her?" he asked.

"I did," I said.

"Did you see her walk through walls?"

"No, I didn't," I said. "I guess I thought that if my teachers said she did, then she did."

"How did she do it?" he asked. I saw that everyone seemed very interested.

"Well, I'm not exactly sure," I replied, "but what people said was that she concentrated so carefully that her molecules all dissolved and she could pass through walls and reconstitute herself on the other side."

Everyone nodded as if that seemed reasonable. The questioner seemed content, and so the conversation continued on to questions about how to concentrate. We did some Mindfulness exercises, some sitting still with eyes closed, some standing and moving. Everyone seemed pleased. I had a good time.

Three days later a large envelope arrived in my mail with twenty-six thank-you letters. Twenty-five began, "Dear Sylvia," one began, "Dear Grandma," and all of them were very enthusiastic and thoughtful, citing particular parts of my presentation.

"I especially enjoyed when we stood up and did Mindfulness moving around."

"I liked the stories you told about the Buddha."

"What I've been thinking about is how I can tell that I'm not paying attention when I'm not paying attention."

One letter said:

Dear Sylvia,

Thank you for coming to visit our class. I enjoyed everything you said. But I'm still thinking about that woman who concentrated so hard she could walk through walls. And I've been wondering, what if she got distracted in the middle of walking through the wall? Would she get stuck in the wall forever?

Yours truly,

Robert

I loved Robert's letter. In addition to being charmed by his uncomplicated, nonchallenging, but nevertheless sincerely interested curiosity, I was delighted by his image of the perils of distraction. I realized how frequently *I* get stuck in walls! I get stuck in walls of lust or desire, thinking, "If only things were otherwise, then I would be happy." Or I get stuck in walls of anger and resentment when things don't go my way. If I'm not careful, I then begin to create scenarios of ever-so-subtle revenge, which further fatigue my mind, and ultimately—when I realize what I have been doing—humiliate me because I am, actually, a nice person.

Every day I bump into "mind walls," walls that *feel* solid because the impact is painful. Only when I remember that the walls are the habits of my own mind, that *I* built them and they will continue to exist as long as I insist that they are real, can I stop building. Then my mind relaxes and I see clearly. I see that the walls are empty, and then I walk right through them.

I also admired Robert's Determination. He persisted as long as his mind was confused. Sometimes, when I'm teaching far from home and people know me only through my books, someone will ask, "How does it feel to have a clear mind all the time?"

I respond, "I wish I knew!"

My mind, like everyone else's mind, falls into habitual, predictable traps. I get confused. Practice is not about never getting trapped. It's about recognizing traps and choosing freedom. If I pay attention, I won't get stuck forever. I'm determined to do it.

STRIVE ON WITH DILIGENCE

The Buddha was an old man, past eighty years old, when he died. On the evening he died, knowing that he was dying, he preached for the last time, encouraging his monks to continue on steadfastly with their practice after he was gone. The Buddha's words, translated into modern idiom, reassure—"I was only able to point the way for you." He also said, "Be a lamp unto yourself!" reminding them, and I think us as well, that we need to see the truth for *ourselves* for it to free us from confusion—and that we can!

I imagine the scene twenty-five hundred years ago with all of the monks gathered around the Buddha, anticipating with sorrow his impending death, and simultaneously being roused and inspired and encouraged. He reminds them that "everything that has a beginning ends," which seems to me both the core of his teaching and—in that moment—a consolation.

The Buddha's final words, often translated as "Strive on with diligence," have an echo of exhortation about them. I find them thrilling. Those words connect me with a sense of faith and confidence in the possibility of freedom that I think the Buddha must have aroused in his followers. I imagine him saying, "Move with sureness into the future."

For many years I taught Mindfulness at Elat Chayyim, a retreat center in the Catskill Mountains of New York, every October. It's a great pleasure for a Californian for whom the seasons don't change very much to see signs of an oncoming real winter: the leaves changing color, many of the trees already bare, and birds, great flocks of them, flying south. Elat Chayyim seems to be in the flyway of geese, and they honk as they go by. I watch them. I notice who the lead goose is, the one I think is giving instructions for synchronized flying. I wonder how those instructions are transmitted, because the squadron shifts direction all at once. Sometimes when I see the flock shift suddenly east or west, sometimes even north, I think to myself, "Go south, go south!" Then I think, "They don't need my help."

The geese turn by themselves, all together, probably in response to an internal signal that they're going the wrong way. They know where they're going. They'll get there. They'll stay awhile. Then they'll fly north. They're always traveling. They never finish. Neither do we.

When I began spiritual practice in the 1970s, my friends and I believed we would become—once and for all—enlightened. I think we were inspired by the Buddha's own enlightened vision and the words he spoke when he understood the mechanism by which the mind—in confusion—weaves individual experiences into an ongoing, seemingly unbroken narrative of a life in which one finds oneself cast as the author of the drama, the principal player, and the hero and victim of everything that happens. Realizing that the sense of owning that role is illusion—and that the role itself is burdensome, frightful to play—the Buddha was able to stop. He said, "The ridgepole is broken. House builder, you will build no more!" He knew he had destroyed, forever, the habit of rebuilding the sense of a separate self. He was free.

I have moments in which I understand that there is no one who owns the narrative of my life, no one to whom the events of my life are happening, that all of creation is a huge, interconnected, amazing production of events unfolding in concert with each other, connected to each other, dependent on each other, with no separation at all. When these moments happen, I feel happy, at ease, and grateful. I think of them as experiences of enlightenment. They are real and I trust them, but they don't last. However clearly I see, however much I think, "Now I will *never* lose this perspective," my mind makes wrong turns and I do lose it.

When I discover that I am—once again—confused, I try to remember that the habit of return is what matters. I credit myself with the insights I've had and assume that I can get them back. I think about the Buddha charging his monks with the responsibility to go on by themselves. I think about the geese, programmed for their journey, and I imagine that we are programmed for our journey as well. I pay attention. I make course corrections. I think about "Strive on with diligence" or "Move with sureness into the future," and I remember that I don't need to move into the whole of the future. Just the next step.

IT'S HARDER THAN YOU CAN IMAGINE: EVERYDAY DETERMINATION PRACTICE

Soon after *It's Easier Than You Think* was published, I began to think about writing a companion volume called *It's Harder Than You Can Imagine*. I wanted to say that understanding how the habits of our minds create suffering doesn't automatically change those habits. I wanted to talk about how persistent those habits are, and how steadfast and disciplined a person needs to be to begin to make a dent in them. I wanted to say that just as my computer suddenly, apparently at its own whim, slips into a font I don't want to use anymore, my mind, unguarded, falls into old patterns. I don't fight with my computer when it slips. And I try not to fight with my mind. I know that when I am paying attention, my mind stays clear and my heart stays open. That is my experience. I am certain that my own good heart is one mind-moment and one breath away. So I start over.

That's the practice for you as well. Plan to be starting over, all the time. Each time you find that your mind has gotten stuck in a struggle, remember that you know the way out. You've found it before. Stop. Take a breath. Dismiss dismay, if you can, as fast as it arises. It's not supposed to be different. This is the way it is. It's easier than you think, *and* it's harder than you can imagine. Freedom from habit is a possibility. Not once and for all, as far as I can tell, but day after day, little by little, and more and more often.

CHAPTER NINE

Lovingkindness

/ /

Free from greed, hatred, and delusion,
alert and mindful,
one pervades first the east,
then the west,
the north,
and then the south,
with abundant, expansive, immeasurable goodwill.
With the strength of a conch-trumpet blower,
without any difficulty,
goodwill fills the all-encompassing cosmos.
—THE BUDDHA

LOVINGKINDNESS

The practice of:	Develops the habit of:	By:	And is supported by:	And manifests as:
Lovingkindness	Well-wishing	Celebrating positive qualities in other people, cultivating forgiveness	Remembering that since suffering is universal, everyone is motivated by the desire to be happy (the First Noble Truth)	Kindness

If I make blessing my habit, if I meet each moment with equal benevolence, my mind relaxes and all of my rehearsed reasons for resenting are redeemed by goodness. The relief of not using categories of affection— "Most Favorite," "Semi-Favorite," "So-So," "Not really," and "Not at all"—as criteria for kindness invites my mind, for its own benefit, to forgive. Being on good terms with all of my life allows me to feel safe and convinces me that Lovingkindness must be the universal antidote to suffering, that it must be what everyone wants most.

LOVINGKINDNESS MEDITATION

I imagine that if the Buddha preached the Loving-kindness Sermon today, that the newspaper article reporting the event would say:

Three Discoveries Ensure Lasting Peace

1. Wholesome living is the cause of happiness.
2. Personal happiness cultivates the insight *"Everyone wants this!"*
3. Human beings have the capacity—"in gladness and in safety"—to wish, unconditionally, "May all beings be happy!"

Commentators would point out that the Loving-kindness Sermon has no special instructions for a wish to make for people you don't like. It doesn't need them. It assumes that one's own boundlessly safe and happy heart has no walls with hooks on them on which to hang old animosities, no filing systems filled with fear stories that get in the way of forgiving.

In Lovingkindness meditation, steadfast well-wishing concentrates the mind, dispelling any barrier to benevolence. The Pali word for Lovingkindness is *metta*, and my colleague Guy Armstrong says that "the *metta* mind" is like frozen orange juice. Everything extra is squeezed out of it. What remains is the essential goodness, only sweeter.

Begin now. Make yourself comfortable. Take a deep breath. Relax. Try to smile. The Buddha taught that there is no other person in the whole world more worthy of your well-wishing than yourself. I love that teaching! It's so kind. And it makes so much sense. When I am unhappy—tense, frightened, tired, or irritable—I think, "Of course! Who else could I *possibly* wish well to? I can't see past myself. I need to feel better first."

Start with yourself. These are the words I am saying these days, so—until you find others more resonant for you—I invite you to try them. Say them out loud, if you're alone. Otherwise, think them.

May I feel protected and safe.
May I feel contented and pleased.
May my physical body provide me with strength.
May my life unfold smoothly with ease.

Now say the phrases again. This time, stop after each phrase and take a deep breath in and out. Close your eyes as you take the breath and experience how that wish feels in your body. Then make the next wish and experience how that one feels. When you know the wishes by heart, close your eyes and say them over and over. Pay attention to how good it feels to wish yourself well. Later on you'll wish for other people. For now, just wish for yourself. For as long as you like. And, really, do try to smile.

TELLING GOOD STORIES

If the traditional list, the Benefits of *Metta*—a list I ask students to memorize, as inspiration, in advance of beginning their formal *metta* practice—were used as advertising copy for a product sold on television, everyone would send away for it.

> People who practice *metta*
> Sleep peacefully,
> Wake peacefully,
> Dream peaceful dreams.
> People love them,
> Angels love them,
> Angels will protect them.
> Poisons and weapons and fire don't harm them.

Lovingkindness

Their faces are clear.
Their minds are serene.
They die unconfused.
And when they die, their rebirth is in heavenly realms.

Just thinking about the list—not even saying it—makes me happy. As an advertisement—without a lot of small-print disclaimers—it's outrageous. As an exuberant, poetic declaration of the ability of the human heart to rest, untroubled, by loving unconditionally, it's gorgeous. "People love them" is the operative line. They are protected by their own lovingness. They are safe.

I recall standing in the kitchen of my son Peter's mother-in-law on the afternoon our families first met and hearing her say, as she pointed out the window at family members arriving for dinner, "Here comes my son Jorge. He is a sweet man—sensitive, a lovely poet. I love him so much!" and "Here comes my daughter Natalia. She is so energetic, so lively, I know you'll love her!" Over time, as we got to know each other, I realized that it is Noemi's habit to mention people by saying their name and including a mini-story about them. I had the feeling that people were filed in her mind by mini-story. I soon noticed that even when the person she spoke about was difficult—"My relative So-and-So was always very critical and demanding but, you know, she had a hard life and she raised her children alone"—she had a tremendous ability to keep the story good. I also noticed that it was a pleasure to be with her.

Paying attention supports the telling of good stories. In Dharamsala, India, in 1995, the twenty-six Western Buddhist teachers who gathered there for a conference with the Dalai Lama arrived two days before the formal meeting to plan the agenda. I realized, looking around the room as we met for the first time, that there were people there I knew and liked, people I hadn't met before, and one person I knew and did not like. She had been quite critical of me at other meetings and I had felt insulted.

My friend Jack, the facilitator of that meeting, suggested, "Let's go around the room and introduce ourselves by saying our name and the largest spiritual challenge facing us in our personal lives and in our work. I'll go first," he said, and began. I could not have imagined a more intimate, vulnerable-making question to ask a group of relative strangers. I knew—since at that time, in Dharamsala, it seemed my largest challenge—I would not be able to avoid saying, "I am a Buddhist and I am also a practicing Jew and I am worrying about whether that will be okay with all of you." I suddenly felt acutely aware of being on a mountaintop, thousands of miles from home.

There was nothing I could do but pay attention. People began to talk. One after another, people told their stories. Everyone's challenge was unique, but everyone had a challenge. Each person's sharing was a thread of our common wish to be clear, to be content, to choose wisely, to feel accepted. When I thought about the experience afterward, I realized that as people spoke, the group changed from people whom I did or didn't like to people like me. As the person I remembered as critical of me was speaking, I noticed that I was feeling the same about her—touched by both her story and her candor—as I had about the person who had preceded her. I was also aware, as the person after her spoke, of what a relief it had been to have listened without filling my mind with memory-banked stories of what she might or might not have said on some past occasion. I liked myself, in that moment, for not being a teller of bad stories. I felt the pleasure of being protected by my own Lovingkindness. When the microphone came to me and I said my truth, it was easy. I think, in retrospect, that it was easy because I'd kept my mind like a good neighborhood, one that it's safe to come out in.

WRITING NEW ENDINGS FOR OLD STORIES

In August of 2001 I woke up to hear the news that a Palestinian suicide bomber had blown himself up in a pizza restaurant in the middle of Jerusalem during the lunchtime rush, killing thirteen people, many of them infants. I felt tremendous despair. I remembered being on the phone several months earlier, on Yom ha-Shoah (Holocaust Remembrance Day), with my friend Ruth, a rabbi spending her sabbatical year in Israel. Ruth had said, "It's completely weird. I am sitting here in my apartment, watching a hope-filled ceremony being broadcast live from Yad Vashem [The Holocaust Museum in Jerusalem], and at the same time I can hear Israeli mortar shells screeching by overhead, aimed at Palestinian targets. I can't figure out," she said, "how this can ever possibly end." Neither of us could have imagined the escalation of conflict that was to follow in 2001, the increased dismay we would all feel over "how this can ever possibly end."

Most commentary that I read about the situation in

the Middle East or any other conflict-plagued place in the world seems focused on what mistakes were made, who made the mistakes, and who was originally to blame—as if there were a single point of origin before which there were no troubles. Even if it were ever possible to know the answer to the question "Who started this fight?" it would not solve the problem of needing to know, "What should we do now?" All of the great spiritual traditions teach that the "enemy" needs to be befriended, that retaliation is endless.

In the Dhammapada, a compilation of the teachings of the Buddha, it says:

> Hatred will never cease by hatred,
>   Only love will erase hatred,
>   This is the eternal law.

Befriending one's enemy, though, however crucial it is to ending hatred and conflict, to reclaiming our own heart's ability to love, is counterintuitive. Befriending requires forgiving, and we are often too frightened to forgive. There must be a mechanism deeply embedded in our brain that keeps the memory of past pain sharply alive in order to protect us from having it happen again. We remember who frightened us in our lifetimes and very likely—through stories, through the gene pool, through racial memory—who frightened our parents and their parents in their lifetimes. Because feeling guilty is frightening, we also remember when we felt ashamed of ourselves because of what we did or of our kin because of what they did. We remember fear in our cells—alerted by adrenaline—long before our mind and our heart get a chance to think. For forgiveness to happen—for our natural inclination to Lovingkindness to emerge—we need to stop frightening each other. We need to feel safe.

Gustav, my study partner at a monthlong intensive Hebrew-language course in Netanya, Israel, in 1995, invited me to come home with him for the two-day Sabbath school break. Gustav is German. He and his wife belong to a religious Christian community that had, after World War II, developed programs in Israel to serve Holocaust survivors. Gustav is the director of a home for elderly survivors who have no relatives. In conversation class he would explain, in careful, competent Hebrew, how both the work that he did and his intention to continue to live in Israel were the motivation for his language studies.

The drive to the old-age home took several hours. We stopped on the way, in Haifa, in front of a small apartment complex. "There is a woman who lives here that I visit every week," Gustav said. "She will need to move to the home soon, but she isn't quite ready. Please wait here for me. I can't take you in with me. Strangers are hard for her."

Alone in the car, I thought about the woman in the apartment and about how I, a Jewish woman, was more of a stranger to her than her young German visitor. Forty-five minutes later Gustav was back.

"I'm really worried about her," he said. "She doesn't see well, and her balance isn't good. It's hard for her to give up the apartment, though—it's so familiar. But I know she looks forward to my visits. I think that when she does move it will be easier for her because she knows me."

It was midafternoon when we finished the drive. The dining room, as we passed through it on the way to my room, was empty. The tables, covered with white cloths, were arranged in a large U shape with chairs on all sides. I knew that eight German adults—some, like Gustav, part of families with children—lived in the building with ten elderly Jews. We would all eat together. Gustav told me that the coordinator of his religious community's many projects in Israel, a man who lived in Jerusalem, had been invited for the weekend, and that a rabbi from Tel Aviv, who would conduct Sabbath services the next morning, was also expected.

Gustav showed me the shelf at the side of the dining room, already set with candlesticks and candles to be lit just before sunset. "If you didn't bring your own," Gustav said, "we have extra."

When I returned to the dining room an hour later, people were gathering at the tables. Some of the candles had been lit. I lit mine. Gustav was playing the guitar softly, a traditional chant for welcoming the Sabbath, "Shalom Aleichem, Malachei ha-Shalom" (Welcome, Angels of Peace). He nodded for me to take the empty seat near his, and I sat down. I saw that the seats had been designated so that the whole community was mingled together—young German, old Jew—all around the table. Every man in the room was wearing a yarmulka (traditional head covering). I realized as I looked around the table that although everyone—other than the three weekend visitors—lived in the building, we all had dressed for the occasion.

A very old man, at the far end of the table from me, stood up to say the ritual blessing over the wine. He had been sitting in a wheelchair and needed to be supported by the people on either side of him. His hand shook as he held his glass. His voice was low, barely audible.

When he finished, he took a sip of his wine and sat back down.

I looked around the room. I saw young Germans, all of them born decades after World War II, and old Jews, trusting the last part of their now enfeebled lives to them. I thought about the mysterious path of forgiveness and about how, without erasing, we can sometimes mend a story by writing more at the end of it. I thought about how long it might take to do the writing.

People began to pick up their wineglasses. Across the table from me, the program coordinator from Jerusalem raised his glass to acknowledge the old woman sitting next to me.

"*Shabbat shalom*" (I wish you Sabbath peace), he said.

The old woman raised her glass in response. "*Shabbat shalom.*"

THE FREEDOM TO FORGIVE

One of the stories told about the origin of Lovingkindness practice is that the Buddha taught it, as a protection, to monks who were frightened because they were about to go off by themselves into the jungle to meditate. Perhaps those monks were comforted, having heard the legend of how a rampaging elephant stampeding into the Buddha's path was brought to his knees by the force of *metta* that surrounded the Buddha. I imagine they believed that same force would ward off tigers and snakes and every other fear-provoking thing they might encounter on their own. I also think *metta* is a protection. But I don't think it's an amulet. Tigers and snakes and fearsome things are wherever they are, doing whatever they do. The miracle protection is the spontaneous Lovingkindness response of the heart to fearsome things seen clearly and fully understood in a mind awakened by mindful attention.

A man named Bret, a novice meditator, told me his story on the last day of a seven-day Mindfulness retreat. He said, "I've been transformed by this retreat. I've never been on a retreat before and I've never even meditated before, and I had no idea it would be like this. But I read about meditation in *Time* magazine and I saw that it's a big thing these days and I figured I should try it. When I came here a week ago the first thing that happened as I began to be in silence and pay attention was that a terrible, traumatic memory of something that happened to me four years ago—a memory that I had managed to lock away somewhere in my mind so I wouldn't have to think about it—came back to me. I thought, 'Uh-oh, here comes this story that I've tried to avoid for four years, and now I've got this whole week stretching out ahead of me and it doesn't look like there's going to be much of an opportunity to avoid it.' So then I thought, 'As long as I'm here, I might as well pay attention to it.'"

"Do you want to tell me that story?" I asked.

He said, "Yes, I do."

This is the story he told me. He said, "I was coming home through a neighborhood where I shouldn't have been walking alone late at night. It's really dangerous to be there. I should have known better. Suddenly, a man jumped out from behind a building, obviously very high on drugs, and he had a gun. He held the gun at my chest and said, 'I'm going to kill you. Give me what you have.'

"Of course I immediately gave him my wallet. It had a lot of money in it—six hundred dollars. There was no question, though—I handed it over. But then he kept the gun at my chest, waving it back and forth. He kept saying, 'I'm going to kill you, I'm going to kill you.' I saw that he was very confused. He seemed to be saying 'I'm going to kill you' over and over in order to get up the nerve to do it. I was terrified. I said, 'Wait! Stop! I'll give you something that's very good.' He stopped. I gave him my watch. And then he started all over again, menacing me: 'I'm going to kill you, I'm going to kill you.' I said, 'Wait! Stop!' and he stopped, but I didn't have anything else to give him. So I said, 'Listen to me! You did *very* well. You did *great!* You have no *idea* how much money is in that wallet. And that watch is worth a lot. When you go home, your friends are going to be *so* proud of you. They're going to think you did really wonderfully. *Now go home.*' And the man turned around and left."

Even as I saw Bret in front of me, alive and apparently well, I felt relieved. His story, four years after the event, was still frightening to hear.

I said to Bret, "How did you know to say that?"

He said, "I don't know. I was terrified, but my mind was very focused. It just came out of me."

The thought passed through my mind (where the image of Bret's assailant, wildly intoxicated, was still vivid) that unconditional appreciation—"You did great!"—is probably the universal, lifesaving password for human connection.

Bret continued his story. "So what happened to me as I began to sit," he said, "is that I would be sitting and the memory of that experience would come up in my mind and it would play through like a movie—I said, he said, I said, he said—and I would shake terribly and feel as terrified as ever. Over and over the memory would come back, and I would feel myself shaking, and I would remember the meditation instructions and try to breathe and pay attention. I didn't try to think about something else. I didn't try to do anything except feel how I felt, and after the whole story would finish playing itself out, I would relax and feel regular and sometimes think, 'Maybe that's it. Maybe it's all finished,' and then the story would start all over again and I'd feel frightened again. Then," he said, "two days ago it started to feel like a horror movie that I'd seen so many times that I knew where the bad parts were. I knew it turned out okay, so the story could replay and I didn't shake. I remembered the whole story, and I realized that I *had* been terrified but didn't feel terrified now. I felt much better.

"Yesterday," Bret continued, "something new happened. The whole movie replayed in my mind. But I was relaxed, and suddenly I thought, 'That man who attacked me was doing what he was doing because he had the life that he had before that. And I was me because I had the life that I had. And if I had had his life, I would have been him, doing what he was doing. And if he had had my life, he would have been me, being

⁓⁓⁓

me. When I realized that, I forgave him. Then I felt *much* better.

"Do you think," Bret asked, "that was an insight?"

I said, "I do."

When I said that to Bret, I was thinking about his profound understanding of the truth of karma, that everything that *ever* happened is responsible for this moment. I could have also been thinking about his realization that paying focused, balanced, nonresistant attention—even when the mind is filled with terror—generates wise response. Or I could have been thinking about his discovery that his heart, freed from fear, was able to forgive. Or that in the end it's forgiveness that saves our lives.

"THANK YOU" AND "IT'S OKAY"

My friend and teaching colleague John Travis told me he had arranged to meet Thubten Yeshe Rimpoche in Katmandu in 1965, because he'd heard that the Dalai Lama was especially recommending him as a teacher for Western students. John said that Lama Yeshe (*lama* and *rimpoche* both mean "teacher") greeted him by saying "Thank you." Lama Yeshe spoke very good English, so he knew that "Thank you" was not a greeting phrase. He apparently said "Thank you" to everything. John understood it as the central message of his teaching: "Whatever is arriving, I can see it most clearly and respond to it most effectively if I am not in contention with it."

"Renouncing contention was Lama Yeshe's practice," John said. "His thanking was a way of keeping himself from getting frightened. I completely got it," John said, "that things happen, that not everything is what you want, that some things you need to change, but that it's all part of life, and that it is manageable. Workable."

I remember once, very early in my practice years, one of my teachers telling a similar story about the dying-breath sentence of an old woman respected for her wisdom. She said, "Thank you very much." I wondered if I would be able to say that too. I thought about a young friend of mine who wrote, in a letter to his friends not long before he died, "I would have wanted more, but I never wanted other." I thought I probably would end up wanting more, and I knew I often wished I had other. I thought about what it might feel like to say a complete "Thank you." I know it would mean renouncing every bit of contention. It would mean forgiving life. For everything. Once, on retreat, feeling—in a

moment of great gratitude—the pleasure of remembering all of my life without any resentment, I said to my
teacher, Jack, "I see that this is really the Practice of the
Well-Tempered Heart. You need to be able to say 'Thank
you' to everything!" I remember Jack looking at me,
head tilted to the side, eyebrows arched in the way that
means he is about to ask me a question to test what I
just said.

"Really?" he said. "What would you say to a
Holocaust?"

I said, "I would say, 'No, thank you.'" He looked at
me. I looked at him. We went on to something else. I
thought we had both left the topic on a shelf of the
mind, that it would come back someday. I said my answer automatically. It *seemed* like the right answer
for the point I was trying to make; probably it was
what I *hoped* was true. But, in truth, I can't thank all
the time. However amazing life is, it is full of pain.
What I know now—more clearly than I did then—is
that not resenting, not being in contention with circumstance, not adding extra suffering to pain, doesn't
require all-out thanking. It only requires accepting. It
requires being able to say, "This is what's true. Okay."
Forgiving is hard practice too, but it's plausible.
Reasonable.

Lovingkindness

I met a woman recently whose practice was making things okay. Forty years after Seymour and I left the apartment we'd lived in for the first year of our marriage, the upstairs half of a two-story brown brick duplex in Boro Park, we went back for a visit. It was a whim. We were spending five days in New York, staying in Manhattan, and one morning I said, "Let's take the subway to Brooklyn." I dressed in my most modest clothing—long skirt, long sleeves, hat covering all my hair. I knew that followers of a particular Hasidic rebbe, conservative in lifestyle, were now the primary residents of the neighborhood, and I did not want to offend.

Our old street looked as I had remembered it, and our house did too, but there was now a voice intercom next to the buzzers for the two apartments. When I pressed the top button, a woman's voice said, "Hello?"

"I'm here with my husband," I said. "We live in California. We lived in your apartment forty years ago."

"Do you want to come up?"

"We do, if it's all right."

"It's okay. Come on up."

At the top of the stairs we were met by a woman I thought might be ten years older than I was. Her sleeves and her skirt were as long as mine, and her hair was covered by a turban. I introduced myself. She said, "I'm Ruth," and shook hands with me but not with Seymour, since it is the custom for Orthodox women not to touch men outside their family. I looked around at the kitchen, renovated and remodeled and much brighter than I remembered it, and noted the two sinks, a sign that this family had very strict *kashrut* (dietary law) observance. I also noticed that Ruth had been in the middle of eating breakfast when we arrived, and I apologized for inconveniencing her.

"It's okay," she said. "Come in. I'll show you the apartment. I've been here forty years. We must have moved in just after you." Ruth walked us through the dining room, also brighter and more cheerful than ours had been, and into the living room. It was lined wall to wall, ceiling to floor, with bookcases of leather-bound Jewish religious texts. The bookcases were new. In 1955 the walls had been bare, we'd had two armchairs, two tray tables, and a black-and-white TV with rabbit ears on top.

"Is your husband a scholar?" I asked.

"He was," Ruth replied. "He had a business, but he also studied. He died four months ago."

"I'm so sorry," I said. "Was he sick a long time?"

"Not so long—a few months." Ruth paused. "He was not a complainer. If he had complained more, maybe the doctors would have taken him seriously earlier. They could have treated him. He could have lived a while."

"Are you angry?" I asked.

"Not so angry," she answered. "I'm sad. And I'm lonesome a lot. So I sleep late. That's why I'm still eating breakfast." I think Ruth was startled by the sudden intimate exchange. I know I was. She said, "These things happen. Come, I'll show you the rest of the apartment."

The two back bedrooms were where I remembered them to be. Ruth closed the door on the larger one, the one we'd slept in, I think to hide the unmade bed. "This is my exercise room," she said, indicating the smaller room. There was a treadmill in the middle of the room, facing a TV. "I try to walk a few miles every day," she said, "and you have to keep up with the news." I noticed that I was feeling relaxed and very pleased. This seventy-year-old woman was not fitting into any stereotype of older Orthodox women.

We passed framed photos of her three sons and their families in the hallway on our way back to the kitchen. I could tell by their styles of dress and the size of their families that they were not all equally traditionally observant. Ruth watched the way I looked at each photo, one at a time, and then back at the others.

"It's okay," she said. "Everyone's different. Come sit down. Let's have coffee."

I asked about Cynthia and Jack, downstairs neighbors forty years before, and their two small daughters. Ruth said that her children had grown up close friends with the two girls.

"They were always running up and down between the two apartments," she said.

"Was there difficulty," I asked, "about the difference in religious observance? I recall that they were not so strict."

"No. It was fine," Ruth said. "They were good people. The girls are married, and Cynthia and Jack live on Long Island. They came to my husband's funeral."

We sat at the kitchen table and had coffee. "I notice you have a slight accent," I said. "Where were you born?"

"I was born in Hungary."

"Did you get out before the war?" I asked.

"No." Ruth paused. I guessed what she was about to

say. People often pause to give the listener time to prepare for what they now anticipate hearing.

"I was in a camp. With my mother and father and sister. My mother died. But my sister and I survived. She was so sick and skinny with typhus I had to carry her out at the end, but we survived. My father too. I met my husband in a displaced-persons camp. We all came to America together. My father just died a few years ago. My sister lives near here, also in the same apartment all these years. Also had three children. Do you want some more coffee? Tell me something about you. Where do you live in California? Do you work?"

"I do," I said. "I'm a psychologist."

Ruth smiled. "I watch psychologist programs on TV," she said. "Do you give advice?"

"Sometimes I do," I answered, a bit worried now that she might ask for some.

"Well, sometimes I feel so sad, I don't get dressed all day. I don't go outside. But then I think, 'Probably I'll be okay. Maybe tomorrow I'll feel better.' Usually I do. You think that's all right?"

"I do," I said.

"Did you see my vitamins?" Ruth asked, indicating the plastic compartmentalized box filled with pills and capsules, different sizes and shapes and colors, counted out for times and days of the week in front of her on the breakfast table. "I watch a health program on TV. It's called *New Age News*. I got the vitamin catalog from them, and I send away."

"Is your health okay?" I asked.

"It's okay," Ruth replied. "I have a little high blood pressure, but I take pills for it."

"From a regular doctor?"

"Sure, from a regular doctor. I showed him my vitamins, and he said they were okay too."

Before we left, Ruth asked to see a photo of my children and grandchildren. I realized, as I showed my wallet photo, that they all looked California casual, very different from Ruth's neighborhood.

"Very beautiful," Ruth said. "Next time Cynthia and Jack phone, I'll tell them you were here."

As Seymour and I walked through Boro Park on the way to the subway, he said, "You're unusually quiet."

"I'm thinking," I replied.

"I notice you didn't mention anything about being a Buddhist teacher. You said you were a psychologist."

"Well, I am that too."

"Were you worried that she wouldn't get it? Or that she'd be put off by you? Or that she'd think you were an imposter—dressed like her, but in fact . . ."

"I think she would have been fine about whatever I was," I said. "What I felt like an imposter about was presuming to know something real about dealing with pain and loss. I was thinking Ruth could be a Buddhist teacher."

"What if she had asked for advice?"

"I was hoping she wouldn't. The truth is," I said, "she blew me away."

A week later I told the whole story of Ruth in Boro Park to my friend Sheila. Sheila is a rabbi and also often teaches meditation with me. "I was amazed," I said, "by Ruth's kindness. She has a lot she could be mad about, but she isn't. *Without* a meditation practice."

"Ruth has a practice," Sheila said.

I thought immediately of Ruth's lifestyle, complex and demanding in form. "Do you think Orthodoxy made her wise?" I asked.

"No," Sheila replied. "Maybe it helped hold her up, but her practice is staying steady through suffering. She knows about not adding rage to her pain. She's keeping her heart open."

KINDLY FASTEN YOUR SEAT BELTS:
EVERYDAY LOVINGKINDNESS PRACTICE

My *metta* practice—when it is not the saying of structured phrases—has been informed by teachings I had from Chagdud Rimpoche, a venerable teacher in the Tibetan Buddhist tradition, and Jo, who is a regular member of the Spirit Rock Wednesday morning class. I think of both teachings as the Lovingkindness Point of View.

I met with Chagdud Rimpoche only once. I arranged to see him because as part of my meditation practice I'd begun to feel very strong and unusual energies in my body, and my friends told me that Tibetan teachers were especially knowledgeable about esoteric energies. I told him, slowly and carefully because we spoke through an interpreter, the details of my experience. I expected that he would give me instructions in a new meditation technique. Instead, he said, "How much compassion practice do you do every day?" I didn't know how to answer. Then he said, "Go out in the street every day and see the suffering." I thought, "How will I know who is suffering? Does he mean everybody? Probably he does. But then what? And what about my energies?" The interview was over, so

I didn't ask. His instruction, though, "Go out in the street every day and see the suffering," was valuable. At the very least, paying attention to other people is probably a modulator of concentration energies. At the very most, it builds compassion.

Jo's teaching was a comment she offered in a class at Spirit Rock Meditation Center. I had been teaching about Lovingkindness and I'd said, "It's easy to wish well to people you love. It's hard to do it with people you don't like. And we usually overlook neutral people, those we have no opinions about. Anyway," I added, "there are very few neutral people. I think we make instant decisions, usually based on very little data, about whether or not we like people. It's hard not to be partial."

Jo, who has been a flight attendant for United Airlines for more than forty years, said, "No, it isn't. When I look out at the passengers in an airplane and say, 'Fasten your seat belts,' I mean it equally for everyone. They are all in the same airplane and we all need to make this trip together. They all look the same to me."

I think about Chagdud Rimpoche when I am standing in line at the supermarket checkout and remember to wonder about the person before me, "What is the biggest difficulty in her life right now?" When I remember, I wish, "May you be happy. May your pain—whatever it is—be lessened." And I think about Jo as I look around and realize that all of us in line—at the supermarket, at the bank, at the post office, at the ticket window—are moving through this line and that line, day after day and year after year, this difficulty after that, making this trip of life together. And everyone still *looks* different to me, but I know that we all have to fasten our seat belts, just the same, for the trip.

The everyday Lovingkindness practice, good wishes for everyone you pass, can happen on its own as you carry on with the rest of your life. When I decided on the *metta* phrases I would use, I set them to a melody that has a special, private meaning for me and practiced them over and over as a chant. I encourage students to do the same. I tell them, "If you do, you'll find that your chant will become like a song about which you will say, 'I can't get that tune out of my mind.' It will be stuck there, playing in every spare moment, and it will make you happy."

So I invite you to do the same. Pick phrases that you like to say. Pick a melody—one that you know touches your heart—and see if you can make the words fit it.

The phrases that I say fit three melodies that are dear to me. I think that's because I hoped they would. Once you've written your song, sing it to yourself always. You will feel different, and the people around you will feel you differently.

CHAPTER TEN

Equanimity

Go forth, and teach the truth
in the idiom of the people,
for the happiness of many,
out of compassion for the world.
—THE BUDDHA

EQUANIMITY

The practice of:	Develops the habit of:	By:	And is supported by:	And manifests as:
Equanimity	Accepting	Experiencing the happiness of impartiality by paying attention to the whole truth of every moment (practicing Wise Mindfulness, the mind-balancing aspect of the Fourth Noble Truth)	Intuiting and acknowledging that this is a lawful cosmos, just and comforting in its dependability; understanding karma, cause and effect, and interdependence	Compassion

To perfect my Equanimity, I need to accept every experience into my awareness. I cannot refuse to pay attention. Refusing itself, the mind tensing in withdrawal, is suffering. And turning the mind away, refusing to look, would preclude complete and clear seeing. When my mind greets all moments with equal respect, it maintains stature enough to see that causal connections set every experience into its lawful time and place, that everything is always—breathtakingly—the only way that it can be. My heart, resting in Equanimity, can respond with compassion.

EQUANIMITY MEDITATION

I've sometimes taught Equanimity meditation by reminding students of the long-gone TV audience participation program *Sing Along with Mitch*. People in the TV studio and presumably people at home in their living rooms watched and listened as a band at center stage, led by accordionist and conductor Mitch Miller, played the melodies of popular songs. The lyrics were projected on the screen as subtitles, and a bouncing-ball icon moved from word to word so that participants hearing a song for the first time could keep pace with the experience and feel part of it.

I describe the TV program and then I say, "Equanimity meditation is just like that. It's the practice of keeping up, staying in tune with what's happening, and staying balanced, even—maybe even especially— when you are in unfamiliar territory." I like to say that even songs with unusual, unanticipated key changes or words with obscure meanings have harmonies that the composer understands, with beginnings and ends that are connected in a pattern. They aren't random.

I say Equanimity meditation instructions this way: Sit comfortably. Close your eyes. Meet each arriving moment—each breath, or each mood, each thought, or each idea—as the next word of the song that needs to get sung. You can choose what line of the score to sing—breath, mood, thought, idea—and still hear the others in the background. If you relax, you'll be able to say, "Now this" and "Now this" and "Well, this is a surprise, but—look!—I can manage this, too, and just in time to be here for this next experience, now arriving." You don't need to anticipate. If you fumble a moment, let it go. Sight-read the music. Just do now, now.

Sit for as long as you like. This is Equanimity meditation. It's also Mindfulness.

"I COULDN'T BE BETTER"

The most active member—for sure, the most *vocal* member—of my Spiritual Direction Committee is my own heart. The other committee members, people I have chosen as witnesses for one or another piece of my inner life, all love me. I know that. I trust them as holders of my secrets—my worries and my embarrassments, my fears and my guilt—and expect they will support me. They always do. My own heart, at least the part of it in charge of moral inventory, is less merciful. Its principal remark is "You should be doing better!"

"Better than *what*?" I could respond if I were thinking clearly. However much I know that the Buddha said, "There is no one more worthy of your benevolent wishes than you yourself," I keep thinking there is some baseline standard of merit I need to meet.

Rose and Gwen are two regular members of the Wednesday morning class at Spirit Rock whose comments, on one particular day, became known as Rose's Remark and Gwen's Corollary. I had arrived at Spirit Rock only a few minutes before class was scheduled that day and so was hurrying through the parking lot toward the building where the class meets. Rose was also hurrying and caught up with me in time for me to say, "Hi, Rose, how are you?"

"I'm fine," Rose answered. Then, a few steps later, she added, "Well, in fact, I am not sure that the job I have now is going to work out. And I'm worried about my daughter in college. But really, I'm fine." By that time we'd arrived at the meditation room. I took my place in front, gave some instructions, and we all sat quietly. When the meditation period was over, I used the conversation with Rose as an example of the Buddha's teaching about suffering and the end of suffering. I probably said something about the possibility of maintaining a balanced, wise response to the inevitable challenges of life as they arise.

I remember saying, "Maybe we should have 'I'm fine' as the secret password of the Wednesday class. That way, when we meet each other in the supermarket or at the dentist, we could ask, 'How are you?' and respond, 'I'm fine,' and we would all understand that as meaning, 'My life is complex, as is everyone's, and I'm managing.' It would also mean, 'Hello. I recognize you from class.'"

Everyone liked that idea. Then Gwen said, "I have a different response to 'How are you?' Whenever someone says, 'How are you, Gwen?' I say, 'I couldn't be better.'"

Gwen paused a moment for people to think, then smile and nod in agreement. "Because," she said, "I *couldn't* be better. *Ever.*"

We couldn't any of us be better, ever, than how we are. If we could, we would. No one purposely decides to suffer. If I am disappointed or startled or offended or frightened and I give myself a bad time over it, saying to myself, "You should rise above this, Sylvia. If you were

really a spiritual person, your heart would never feel anything but grateful," I compound my pain. I know this,
but I do it anyway.

It might be one of the pitfalls of spiritual practice.
It's an easy trap for me to fall into. I absolutely trust
that I can refine the capacities of my own heart, and
I inspire myself with stories I hear, and then tell,
about people with incredible nobility of spirit. Like
the story of the Zen teacher who, with her very last
breath—in the tradition of Zen teachers who save
their pithiest teaching for their last breath—said, "I
have no complaints." I think about her when I hear
my own mind complaining, annoyed that things
aren't going the way I wanted them to. I know that
not complaining doesn't mean not responding. I also
know I could be proactive with a loving heart. But I
still hear my mind being indignant or self-righteous,
or telling itself sorrowful stories. All bad habits. All
painful habits.

The best possible response to pain—to *any* pain—is
compassion. Maybe the whole of spiritual practice rests
on remembering—over and over again—that we are,
after all, human beings. We want to feel good. We want
not to hurt. We want not to yearn. When we were three
or four years old our parents and teachers began saying

to us, "You don't always get what you want," and we know it's true, that the world *does* work that way. But even though we know, nobility of spirit—all the time—is hard.

Twenty-five years ago when my friend Pat, still a young woman, was dying, she invited her ex-husband and his new wife to Thanksgiving dinner at her house so that her teenage children would be able to make the transition from her home to their new home more easily after her death. Afterward she told me, "You know, not every single thought I had during the day was a good one."

I said, "Pat, you cannot get canonized *before* you die. That happens *after*."

Perhaps my colleagues and I should reconsider the traditional stories we tell to inspire people. Maybe we should tell more believable stories, more like our own experience. Even if we did, though, I'm not sure it would work. We all seem to be much readier to forgive other people, or to encourage them to forgive, than we are to forgive ourselves.

When I supervise people learning to be Mindfulness teachers, I reassure them about their ability to respond to any question a student might ask. I say, "Just assume that the answer to every possible question is

'Compassion.'" I also say, "Try to include a technical answer as well—'Perhaps sit in a softer chair' or 'Keep your eyes open if it makes you more alert'—but remember that every call for help is a plea for compassion. When the heart is at peace—body notwithstanding, outside events notwithstanding—a thanking, grateful, awe-inspired benevolence is all that's left. That heart has no questions."

Everyone agrees. Everyone knows compassion is the right response. The problem, students remind me, is with ourselves, not with other people. They ask—and it could be me asking as well, since knowing the answer does not cure the problem—"What if I am trying to be compassionate with myself, what if I know I could stop suffering if I just forgave myself, and what if I *still* can't do it?"

I tell them—and remind myself—that the human heart has its own built-in, self-healing intent and its own timetable. So far, that's the best I know.

EVERYTHING HAPPENS TO EVERYBODY

It is my custom, one I learned from my teachers, to end Mindfulness retreats with a formal recitation of prayers for the well-being of all beings and a formal Dedication of Merit (a declaration of intent to offer our own well-being on behalf of all beings). They are lovely to say:

May all beings be happy, may all beings be peaceful, may all beings come to the end of suffering.

May whatever merit we accrue from our practice and study together be offered freely and shared with all inhabitants of the earth. May all beings come to the end of suffering.

Over the years of my practice it has become increasingly clear to me that those closing forms are very much more than ringing the final bell, or stacking the mats and *zafus,* or thanking the people who've been sitting next to you for being such staunch supporters. They are faith expressions—the summary response to the questions "What are you doing?" "How do you do it?" "Why do you do it?" and "Is it working?"

We practice to arrive at that heart space of peace in which the well-being of others is as dear as our own, where Lovingkindness and compassion and empathic joy are spontaneous. Saying the ritual phrases, not because it is the time to say them but because we *feel* like saying them, and experiencing the happiness—indeed, the freedom—that inspires that feeling mean it is working.

Given enough space, support, and encouragement, the heart calms down—and wakes up—all by itself. At Spirit Rock, at the Wednesday morning class, we begin with brief meditation instructions and then we sit quietly for forty minutes. I usually have a sense of how much time has passed without looking at my watch. I'll notice, after a while, how much pleasure I feel in my body from how still the room has become. Or I'll notice how some small issue of the day that had been gathering up steam to become a problem before I began to sit has become just a thought, something I know I'll take care of easily. Or I'll notice that a substantial pain in my life—a worry that I brought with me and about which I had thought, "I am distracted and upset. How can I lead this class today?"—has developed some breathing space around it, and my attention, no longer held hostage by fear, is free. On the simplest of days, the signal that we've sat long enough is feeling enormously grateful for a room full of companions who want to share this journey. The confirming sign for me, whatever the particulars of any given day, that my heart has settled back down into itself is that I realize I am thinking about other people and wishing them well.

On some Wednesdays we just sit quietly until I ring the bell. Sometimes I say, "It's almost time to ring the bell. So if you were planning for some *metta* time, for well-wishing prayers for the people in your life, you might want to do that in these next minutes of silence together." And sometimes I mention a name out loud. I might, for example, say, "In these last few minutes before I ring the bell, I am thinking about my friend Mary, who has broken her leg, and I hope you will send wishes for healing for her in your thoughts as well. And I invite you to say out loud the names of the people in your heart, and their special circumstance, so we can join our prayers with yours."

People sit still, eyes closed, and begin—after only the briefest of pauses—to speak names and situations into the room.

"I am thinking of my mother, Eloise, who has macular degeneration."

"I am thinking of my daughter Carol, who just had a second miscarriage."

"I am thinking of my brother Frank, who has lung cancer."

". . . my aunt Laura, with emphysema."

". . . my son John, just diagnosed bipolar."

". . . my neighbor Virginia, whose daughter died in a car accident last Sunday on her way back to college."

I don't call on people to speak. In random order, from different parts of the room, voices speak names, relationships, and special circumstances. Sometimes I recognize a voice or a name, more often not. Sometimes the petitions go on for what seems a very long time. I think no one feels rushed because we've been sitting quietly so long. I think we also share the sense that the mentioning and the listening *is* the prayer so there is no hurry to get finished, no place else to go. After a while, given names seem to fall away.

". . . my grandson, who has ADD."

". . . my sister, who has breast cancer."

". . . my friend with diabetes."

". . . my friend with depression."

". . . my niece, who is anorexic."

". . . my husband's sister, who is dying of a brain tumor."

At some point the room becomes quiet again, and we sit a while longer. I say a blessing for all the people we've mentioned, and for all people suffering everywhere, and I ring the bell. It often happens, then, that we just sit there and look at each other for a while. It feels as if it requires some moments of looking at each other, perhaps taking some fortifying long breaths in and out, before we say, "Okay. Let's talk about it."

What we talk about is how we have reminded each other—once again—of how hard it is to be a human being with a body subject to old age, sickness and death, and relationships that cause us to be dear to one another. My mother, my father, my sister, my daughter, my friend . . . We cannot do other than care—we wouldn't *want* to do other than care—and caring is painful because everyone is losing something, health or youth or vigor or opportunity or someone they love, all the time.

I recall hearing, for the first time, the legend of the young mother rushing with her dead son in her arms to plead with the Buddha—known to have miraculous powers—to restore her child to life. I knew at once, as you will too if you are new to this story, that when the Buddha responded, "I will do it if you bring me a mustard seed from a household in which no one has ever died" that the boy would not come back to life. The mother, disconsolate, returns from her quest knowing that everyone dies and that the heart can survive grief. To me, the "Bring me a mustard seed" instruction means, "Look around you. You are supported by everyone else in the world." And I understand the end of the legend, the mother bowing in sorrowful surrender, as the miraculous healing.

I feel myself supported by everyone else in the world. At Spirit Rock, on those mornings when we say our prayers out loud, when I hear someone whose voice I don't recognize say, "My aunt Claire, who has Parkinson's disease," I remember my friend Claire, who doesn't have Parkinson's disease but has something else, and Phyllis, who does have Parkinson's disease, and my aunt Miriam, who until her recent death was the only person left in my family older than I am. I think something similar happens—with each name, each relationship, each circumstance spoken—for everyone in the room. It feels to me that we connect with each other in shared recognition of the vastness of human suffering, and of the power of affective bonds. My mother, my father, my sister, my daughter, my friend . . .

Not all of the special circumstances that move the heart to prayer are dire. Every Wednesday is different. Most often the petitions begin with difficult circumstances, and after the room has become quiet again, after the pain has been told, someone will say, "I'm thinking of my daughter Jessica, who has just been accepted into three medical schools and needs to choose." Or "I'm thinking of my son and daughter-in-law, who are on their way to Peru to meet their newly adopted baby daughter."

"I'm thinking about my college roommate from Michigan, who has remained my friend for fifty years and who is arriving tonight for a visit."

The murmurs of pleasure and chuckles of delight that greet the hearing of good news, no matter how unique, let everyone know that we are connecting, not by sharing the situation but by recognizing joy.

And sometimes the special circumstances are plainer, more universal.

"My daughter is pregnant."

"My son graduated from eighth grade."

"I'm getting married."

"Today is my birthday."

I think the joys get mentioned spontaneously, without being called for, only after what is most painful and most frightening has been said. It seems as if everyone hears the message "These are the difficult things that happen to people. They aren't anyone's fault. They happen. They are bearable," and the collective, balanced group attention that was able to hold all of the suffering then allows—perhaps invites—the rest of the message: "These other things happen also." On one particular morning when the list of special circumstances had been especially diverse, the kinship connections unusually wide-ranging, and many people had mentioned how other people's prayers had inspired their own, someone said, "Look! Everything happens to everybody."

It does, sooner or later, in permutations or combinations of sorrow and joy that come with this life, these parents, this body, these opportunities. The traditional Buddhist Equanimity meditation, "All individuals are heir to their own karma," serves me as a mind steadier, a reminder that everything that is happening is the result of an incredible complexity of conditioning causes—in fact, of everything that ever happened—and that it is happening to everyone collectively, the legacy of a lawful cosmos in which praise and blame are irrelevant and thanksgiving and compassion are all that make sense.

"ONLY CONNECT":
EVERYDAY EQUANIMITY PRACTICE

E. M. Forster said it in *A Passage to India:* "Only connect." It's the fundamental instruction for Equanimity—spaciousness of mind wide enough to balance life. It's also the instruction for Mindfulness—awakened connection to the moment; focused, *balanced* attention, with all its resources of perception, memory, recognition, reflection, and decision open to Wisdom and capable of response. It's the essential instruction for being meaningfully and wholeheartedly engaged in the world.

On my desk I have a tiny framed photo of my father, with his arm around me, standing next to a telescope at what is clearly a highway pull-off and vista point. The note on the back of the photo reads, "Lookout Mountain, Windham, New York, July 12, 1939." So I am three years old. I know that he and I stood at many similar viewing scopes during my childhood, so I assume that my memory of his instruction for seeing clearly is a conflated one. I remember it as "Look with both eyes, Sylvia. Keep them open. And stand in front of the two lenses. Right here. Otherwise you won't see clearly."

Maybe this was the most important part: "Look *now*," my father would say, "because we'll have to leave soon, and you'll have missed it."

Here is the instruction: Only connect. Wherever you are, right now, pay attention. Forever.

God and the Owls

It was the last morning and the final meditation period of a five-day Mindfulness retreat for rabbis, and I was thinking to myself as I gave the instructions, "You are saying this so well, Sylvia. You're really good at this!"

Just at that moment there was a huge thunderclap, and hail—the kind that when I lived in Kansas used to be described as "big as golf balls"—began rat-tat-tatting on the skylight. Moments before, the day had been sunny and still, and suddenly the wind was whipping around the building and the windows were rattling. I had the fleeting thought, "I wonder if this storm has something to do with my excessive pride."

I looked around. I noticed that Jeff and Sheila, my teaching colleagues, had their eyes closed. Most of the other folks did, too. The people who had opened their eyes were looking out, watching the storm. The intervals between lightning flashes and thunder crashes got shorter; at one point they seemed synchronous, and I thought, "The storm is right over us." I wondered if that meant we were completely safe or completely jeopardized. I looked around again. No one had moved. Everyone seemed content. Some people smiled. Twenty minutes after it had begun, as abruptly as it had started, the storm stopped and I rang the bell.

The first person to speak said, "I had been preparing to say, as my closing remark, 'What a fine group of three teachers we've had all this week.' Now I remember that we had four."

A ripple of pleasure slid through the room as everyone appreciated both the religious sentiment and the fact that it didn't require further explication.

Four hours later I was buckled into my seat on an American Airlines flight from Newburgh, New York, to Chicago, waiting for takeoff. It began to seem like a long time since the plane had taxied from the gate and moved into the line of departing flights. Finally the captain's voice on the intercom announced, "We're being delayed, folks. You may have noticed those dark clouds that have come up in the last few minutes. What's happening is that cold air from Canada is meeting warm, moist air from the Caribbean, and it's producing a north-south band of violent storms that are now halfway between here and Chicago. Those of you who were in the Newburgh area this morning experienced a very similar band of storms as it passed through here earlier."

"A meteorological explanation," I thought, "replacing the theological one."

Thirty more minutes passed; the captain kept us updated. "Maybe we are going soon," and then, "Maybe not. We're still waiting." I exchanged some pleasantries with my seatmate, and then we both overheard the conversation of the two people sitting in the seats in front of ours. Apparently they were also traveling alone, strangers to each other.

"I've been here in Newburgh for a week," a woman's voice said. "My mother died. She was old, eighty-seven, and she still lived in her own home, the same one I grew up in. All my sisters—I have five of them—came from all over. We had the funeral on Monday, but we needed the whole week to get the house empty and ready to sell."

A man's voice responded with words of condolence.

"No, it's really been fine," the woman continued. "It was good for all the sisters to be together. We don't get to see each other often. And this way we went through all my mother's things together, and everyone got to pick what they wanted.

"I'll tell you what, though," she went on. "You see this storm? Well, this morning we finished cleaning up the whole house. Everyone had taken what they wanted. We'd given the rest away. The only things left were the owls. My mother collected owls. God knows why. She just did. Wooden owls. Little pewter owls. China owls. She'd been doing it for years. She had a big collection. None of us wanted them. All week long I was trying to figure out what to do with them. Finally, this morning, I decided I would give them away, and I made a phone call to arrange to have them picked up. That very minute the thunder and lightning started. I *knew* it was my mother letting me know she was mad about the owls!"

The plane taxied back to the gate, and I spent the night in a motel in Newburgh. I thought about the way in which the mind takes what's happening and makes a story out of it—"It was to teach me," or "It was to punish me," or even "It was an omen." Of all the explanations offered for the thunderstorm, the cold air meeting warm, moist air seemed the least personal, the least egocentric. It was raining on millions of people impartially. Still, it didn't supply an answer for why the cold front was moving down on that particular day and whether the unusual weather for late spring—fierce winds and huge hail—was the consequence of global warming, itself the consequence of too much burning of fossil fuel, itself the consequence of . . .

The Buddha named karma, the cause-and-effect relationship of everything in existence, as one of the "imponderables," something that could be intuited as valid, therefore eliciting the response of care and kindness, but not figured out by the rational mind. Ajahn Sumedho uses a wonderful phrase for encouraging the mind to directly experience the moment, without elaboration. He says, "I say to myself, 'It's like this.' It's just what's happening."

Stories with hypothetical explanations are sometimes fun—"The cosmos arranged to have you miss your plane just so that you could take *this* plane and meet *me*"—but still, they're just stories. I recently stayed five minutes later than I'd meant to at Spirit Rock, talking with someone who'd come with a problem they wanted especially to ask me about, and when I arrived at the Golden Gate Bridge on my way into San Francisco, I came upon a serious accident that seemed just to have happened. For a moment I thought, "Ah, I am being rewarded for the kindness of staying late to help someone." That idea followed the thought that I had missed this accident by only five minutes and five miles. Then I realized that I had also just missed every *other* accident happening in the whole world. By more minutes, more miles, perhaps even because I was on the other side of the earth—but just because I was where I was and the accident was where it was. *It's like this*. Not because of me or in spite of me. And I was glad to have spent the five extra minutes at Spirit Rock and hoped I had been helpful.

I imagine that sometime soon someone will publish an anthology of cartoons of the last quarter century with the image of a guru sitting cross-legged at the mouth of a mountaintop cave speaking to a spiritual aspirant, huffing and puffing from the arduous climb, seated across from him. The captions—variations of "Life is a river" or "Maybe life is a river" and often "Life is a lesson"—are responses to the implied question "What is the meaning of life?" Perhaps the ultimate answer was the cartoon caption in an April 2001 issue of *The New Yorker:* "If I knew the meaning of life, would I be sitting in a cave in my underpants?" What makes the guru-on-a-mountain cartoons so enduringly funny is not particular answers. It's the question.

"What is the meaning of life?" does not solve the problem of "What should we do?" A young monk in the Buddha's community is said to have complained that his questions about experiences before birth and after death had not been answered. In response, the Buddha is said to have suggested that the monk consider what would happen if a person, shot and wounded by a poisoned arrow, were to spend time reflecting on the cause of the attack, the probable assailant, or the nature of the poison instead of removing the arrow. Even now, twenty-five hundred years later, the Poison Arrow Parable is a potent, succinct introduction to what the Buddha taught. We often teach the arrow story as part of the explanation of the summary the Buddha is said to have given of all his teaching: "I've come to teach one thing, and one thing only: Suffering and the end of suffering."

Ending suffering depends on seeing clearly, without bias, "It's like this," so the "What should we do?" question can answer itself.

There is a band of violent thunderstorms moving eastward from Chicago.

We can stay in Newburgh overnight.

Life is so difficult.

How *can* we be anything but kind?

Acknowledgments

Leslie Meredith was this book's first editor, and I am enormously appreciative of the very close attention and direction that she gave to the manuscript from its very beginning. Whenever I see one of her lovely stylistic touches in a description I've written, I think, "Thank you, Leslie."

Nancy Miller became the editor of this book when Leslie moved to her new job, and I have been nothing but happy with the smooth, really effortless transition the book made from one set of shaping hands to another. Nancy brought a new perspective to the book that has been a valuable, complementary addition.

Acknowledgments

My friend Martha Ley has been, with this book as with all my others, available for phone calls and e-mails: "Martha, listen to this" and "Martha, read this and tell me what you think." I trust her keen ear, and her support keeps me confident. We have continued our ritual of my reading the whole book aloud to her before the final galleys are returned.

It would be impossible to overstate how glad I am to have my friend Tom Grady as my literary agent. He has been, from our very first meeting, unfailingly attentive, available, thoughtful, generous with editorial suggestions, steadfastly reassuring, and an imcomparable appreciator.

My sons and daughters and all of their families have been, throughout this endeavor as they are for all my endeavors, a source of endless delight, validation, and support. And a share of the merit of this book belongs to my husband, Seymour, who has been, for fifty years now, the love of my life and my best friend.